THE GIANT BOOK OF STRANGE BUT TRUE SPORTS STORIES

THE GIANT BOOK OF
STRANGE BUT TRUE

SPORTS STORIES

BY HOWARD LISS
ILLUSTRATIONS BY JOE MATHIEU

Random House New York

Library of Congress Cataloging in Publication Data

Liss, Howard. The giant book of strange but true sports stories. SUMMARY: True anecdotes from the world of sports — many humorous, all unusual. 1. Sports stories. [1. Sports—Anecdotes, facetiae, satire, etc.] I. Mathieu, Joseph. II. Title. GV707.L57 796'.02'07 76-8132 ISBN 0-394-83287-6 ISBN 0-394-93287-0 (lib. bdg.)

Manufactured in the United States of America

For my nephew, Steve Liss

CONTENTS

Baseball

Auto Racing

Basketball

Boxing

Football

Golf

Hockey

Tennis

Miscellaneous

THE GIANT BOOK OF STRANGE BUT TRUE SPORTS STORIES

BAD-HOP GROUNDERS

A ground ball that takes a bad hop is an infielder's nightmare. Sometimes it can lose a ball game. Once in a while it can even injure the unlucky fielder. In the 1960 World Series, Tony Kubek of the New York Yankees was hit in the throat by a bad-hop grounder. An important run scored and Kubek had to leave the game.

But bad-hop grounders aren't always so serious. In September 1948 the Boston Red Sox were at bat against the Philadelphia Athletics. They had Ted Williams on third and Billy Goodman at bat. Goodman hit a sharp, twisting grounder toward Philadelphia shortstop Eddie Joost.

Joost got in front of the ball, but he couldn't handle it. It hit his glove, ran up his arm and disappeared into the sleeve of his shirt. Joost dropped his glove and began to search all over for the ball. It was under his shirt!

He started to unbutton the shirt, but that was too slow. Finally he pulled his shirttail out of his pants. The ball dropped out and rolled away.

Goodman reached first and then stood on the bag, grinning. Williams, who could have scored easily, was still standing on third base, laughing too hard to run.

Hockey Puck Legends

Books on the history of hockey often try to explain how the game and its equipment were invented. The stories are hard to prove, and even if they are not true, they seem believable. For instance, how was the hockey puck invented?

In the early days of hockey, a lacrosse ball was used. It was almost impossible to control the ball, to pass or shoot it. A hard whack could send it almost anywhere. When the game was played outdoors, players often got a rest while someone chased down the ball.

Then the game moved indoors. One day in an indoor rink players were swinging at the ball with wild abandon. When it flew out of bounds and into the gallery it began smashing windows. Finally, after about $300 worth of windows had been broken, the rink owner had had enough. He seized the ball, took out his penknife and sliced away its top and bottom. All that was left was the round, flat rubber middle of the ball.

"From now on use only this piece!" he roared. The players liked the way they could control it. And that, says the story, is how the hockey puck was invented.

The ice rinks where early hockey was played were always colorful places. They were intended for recreational skating, so there was often music playing, and the rafters of the rink were decorated with bunting and flags.

During one game a player drove in on goal and took a hard swipe at the puck. But he misjudged his swing. Instead of hitting a whizzing line drive, the player golfed the puck high into the rafters. It disappeared in the fluttering bunting. The puzzled goalie looked all around but couldn't find it anywhere.

Then, suddenly, the puck worked itself loose. It dropped down, hit the goalie on the back and rolled into the goal for a score.

In another game a situation arose that could conceivably happen even today.

A terrific shot hit the metal side bar and the puck split in half. One section rolled into the goal while the other slithered away somewhere else.

Was it a goal? Half the puck was inside the goal marker. Was it not a goal? The other half was outside. An argument ensued. How would *you* decide?

The referee judged it a goal scored, and the game continued with a new puck.

The Trade

Istvan Gaal was a young Hungarian soccer player who was unhappy in Hungary. In July 1970, he traveled to Yugoslavia, and from there he fled to Italy. He had dreams of playing professional soccer in North America, so he got in touch with someone from the Toronto team of the National Soccer League. When the Toronto management heard that Gaal had scored 31 goals in 44 games while in Hungary, they were very interested in obtaining his services. Gaal was brought to Toronto.

But John Fischer of the Kitchener soccer team had also heard of Gaal by then. Kitchener was in 13th place in a league that had 14 teams and desperately needed a good player. They followed the young Hungarian. One day Gaal was with a representative of the Toronto team. The representative left him standing on a street corner for a few minutes while he went on an errand. Friends of the Kitchener team drove by, persuaded Gaal to get into their car and then sped away.

Gaal was soon in a Kitchener uniform, but unfortunately he was a big disappointment as a player. He played in one exhibition game and was a substitute in a scheduled game, but he did nothing spectacular.

Toronto had not signed a contract with Gaal, so they could not claim he was their property. But when they heard that Kitchener was about to drop him, they asked Kitchener to release Gaal to them.

The Kitchener team refused to give a player away free.

"What do you want for him?" Toronto asked.

Fischer thought for a moment, then replied, "I'll give him to you for a soccer ball."

Toronto agreed and made the trade.

Gaal had been brought 3,000 miles by one team, kidnapped and signed by another, then traded back to the first team for a soccer ball.

John Fischer of Kitchener said he was sorry if the trade humiliated Gaal. But he pointed out that a good soccer ball is worth $27.50. And he said that Gaal was not the first athlete to be traded for equipment. Some years earlier a hockey player had been traded for a pair of nets.

WRECKING CREW

Everyone has seen karate exhibitions where men split boards and bricks with the sides of their hands. But the greatest karate exhibition of all time was given at Bradford, England. A team of 15 karate experts demolished a six-room 150-year-old house.

As two hundred spectators cheered them on, the team "attacked" its opponent, the house. They used only their bare hands, their bare feet and their bare heads. Several of the experts were used by their teammates as battering rams.

It was a very strong house. Most troublesome of all was the fireplace. Phil Milner, the team leader, said admiringly, "It was a very well-built house and a worthwhile challenge. We must have toppled over three tons of the house in one go."

When the house was reduced to rubble, the whole team faced the ruins and bowed. This was the traditional ceremony to honor a "defeated opponent."

The ARAB BOWL

New Year's Day is the traditional date for football bowl games: the Rose Bowl in Pasadena, the Cotton Bowl in Dallas and others. On New Year's Day, 1944, a most untraditional bowl game was played, perhaps the strangest bowl game ever.

To begin with, the bowl game was not played in the United States but in Oran, North Africa. The spectators were not pennant-waving college students and graduates. They were American soldiers and sailors (many of them recovering from wounds), some French soldiers and a number of Arabs. And the game itself was the first and only *touch football* bowl game in history.

As 1944 opened, the United States was deeply involved in World War II. Of the millions of Americans overseas, many thousands were in North Africa, which had been freed from Axis control during 1943.

Staging an Arab Bowl game was Sgt. Jim Harrigan's idea. Harrigan was sports editor of the military newspaper *Stars and Stripes.* He made his plans for the game with Cpl. Zeke Bonura, a former first baseman for the Chicago White Sox. Officers from army and navy headquarters agreed the game was a good idea, but then came all the military red tape and the arguments.

It happened that several units stationed in North Africa had formed a kind of North African Football Conference. The two top teams of this "league" wanted to play in the "Arab Bowl." Other officers and men wanted a game between the army and the navy men instead. Finally, Harrigan and Bonura suggested a compromise. Why not have a football doubleheader? The first game could be played by the Casablanca Rab Chasers and the Oran Termites, for the North African Football Conference championship. The second game would be between the Army all-stars and the Navy all-stars. That seemed to satisfy everybody.

Both services wanted to win that game. Staffs at their headquarters looked through service records of men who were in or near North Africa, to find out who had played football in high school or college. Several such players received special orders to come to Oran. They had time for a couple of weeks of practice before the game.

January 1, 1944, was a very hot day in Oran. In a rugged opening game, the Casablanca Rab Chasers defeated the Oran Termites for the North African Conference championship.

And now another problem arose. Neither of these teams would loan their equipment for the "Army-Navy" game. Shoulder pads and jerseys were so hard to get that they were too valuable to lend to strangers.

After hurried consultation with the players, the admirals and the generals, Zeke Bonura made an announcement over the public-address system.

"We have a problem with equipment," he told the crowd. "Now, we can't have tackle football without shoulder pads. So this will be a touch football game." The spectators groaned. "But," Bonura went on, "blocking will be permitted. Also, we will now present the between-games entertainment."

There were some loud sounds passing as music, and several service bands came onto the field. Then came camel and burro races, with members of the Women's Army Corps (called WACs) and Red Cross nurses mounted on the animals. The selection of the beauty queen was the highlight. Three WACs were entered, but each received so many cheers that the contest was declared a tie. The Arab Bowl had three queens.

The army and navy teams wore the weirdest assortment of uniforms anyone had ever seen. Some players had football cleats, others wore sneakers. Some players wore jerseys, but no two matched. And most players wore brown T-shirts.

Since nobody had pads, the ground game was mostly end runs. A lot of passes were thrown. Nobody was really hurt by the blocking, but the heat caused many substitutions.

Navy scored on a blocked punt and a pass. The kick was good, to make the score 7–0. Army tied the game before the half ended.

The second half was scoreless until the final minute of play. Army's Eddie Herbert intercepted a pass and returned it to the Navy 20-yard line.

With time for one more play, De Mello place-kicked a perfect field goal, and Army won the game, 10–7.

By the next New Year's Day, nearly all the players and spectators were somewhere else. Many fought in the major battles of 1944. Others were transferred back to the United States. So the Bowl was a one-of-a-kind event. But for the soldiers and sailors far from home, it was a welcome break from the grimness of the war and a happy memory for years after.

BAT-THROWERS

Throwing a bat is one of the most dangerous things a baseball player can do, and umpires usually send a man out of the game for throwing it on purpose. But in at least two cases major league umpires found a different way to handle a bat-thrower.

The Cleveland Indians once had an infielder named Ivy Olson. Olson wasn't much of a hitter. In one game, Olson was at bat, and the count was three-and-two. He watched the next pitch go by, and the umpire called strike three. Olson got very angry. He said a few harsh words to the umpire and then threw his bat high in the air.

When the bat landed on the ground, the umpire calmly picked it up and threw it in the air himself, much higher than Olson had thrown it.

"O.K.," growled the umpire. "You're no good at throwing a bat, and you're no good at judging a ball or strike. Now shut up and sit down or I'll throw you out of the game!"

Some years later, Danny Murtaugh, then playing for Houston in the minor leagues, was in the same situation as Olson. Again the count was three-and-two, and Murtaugh took a called strike three. Murtaugh tossed his bat high into the air. But the umpire of that game had no sense of humor.

"You catch that bat before it lands or I'll fine you twenty dollars," the umpire roared.

Murtaugh judged the flight of the bat and caught it before it hit the ground. He later played in the major leagues and managed the Pittsburgh Pirates to two National League pennants. But he never made a better catch in his life.

GASP!

GAG!

Don't Miss the Bus

A familiar sight to fans who watch distance races is the winner crossing the finish line and almost collapsing. His face is pained, and he is gasping for breath. His legs can scarcely hold him. He has to be supported by friends, who lead him gently off the track.

Emil Zatopek of Czechoslovakia finished races that way. Spectators thought he might even die unless he received oxygen. But it was just an act. Zatopek knew that fans liked to see "the big finish" and he never disappointed them. He found racing fun, and he loved a good joke while running. Once, in an Olympic trial, he took the lead, but then dropped back. When he was far back in the pack, he ran alongside an American runner.

"Hurry up, you'll miss the bus," Zatopek said, and then sprinted into the lead again.

In the 1948 Olympics, when Zatopek was 25 years old, he won the 10,000-meter race and finished second in the 5,000-meter. But in 1952, at Helsinki, Emil Zatopek demonstrated to the world how a great champion could run a race and have fun at the same time.

First he entered the 10,000-meter race (10,000 meters is a little less than six and a half miles). For about 3,000 meters he was content to let someone else set the pace. Suddenly he raced ahead and took the lead. With every stride he seemed about to fall down on the track. Yet when someone came up to challenge, Zatopek promptly ran away from him. He finished first. His time was 29 minutes 17 seconds, beating his own Olympic record by 42 seconds.

"I am disappointed," Zatopek told reporters earnestly. "I wasn't fast at all. I will try to do better in the 5,000-meter race."

In the 5,000-meter race, Zatopek was behind the leaders for a long time. At the 4,000-meter mark, Zatopek made his move. It was an exciting finish. On the last turn the Czechoslovakian took an outside lane and sprinted to the finish line ahead of Algeria's Alain Mimoun. Zatopek broke the Olympic record by nine seconds!

Then Zatopek announced that he would compete in the marathon (the longest distance event—26½ miles). He had never run that event before. When asked how he expected to win, Zatopek replied, "If I didn't think I could win, I would not have entered."

After 15 miles, Zatopek was in the lead. Not far behind was Jim Peters of Great Britain, who had been favored to win. Zatopek dropped back until he was running alongside Peters. The Czech, who spoke several languages, said to Peters, "I have never run a marathon before, but aren't we running a little slow?"

Perhaps Zatopek was trying to discourage the Britisher, or maybe he was having his little joke. A couple of miles later, Peters quit the race because of cramps. Zatopek continued on and won the race, breaking the record by more than six minutes.

When reporters asked him about the marathon, he said, "Really, it's a very boring race."

There is one more incident to report about the 1952 Olympics. Emil Zatopek's wife, Dana, also entered an event, the women's javelin competition.

It was only natural that she would win and also set an Olympic record!

PUFF, PUFF !!

HACK!

COACH'S ORDERS

Coaches expect to be obeyed. Players who don't follow orders often get left out of the game. But on at least one occasion, players' disobedience won a big football game.

In the Rose Bowl game of January 1, 1950 between Ohio State and California, the score was tied at 14–all, with less than a minute and a half left to play. Ohio State had the ball on California's 6-yard line, fourth down, 3 yards to go. Coach Wes Fesler pointed to his kicking specialist Jim Hague and told him to go into the game to try a field goal. Dick Widdoes was also sent in to hold the ball for Hague.

But when the kicker and his holder trotted onto the field, three Ohio State players began to scream at them. "Go back! Go back! We want the touchdown!"

Hague and Widdoes hesitated, unsure what to do. The coach had sent them in, but their teammates were waving them back.

The officials milled around waiting for play to resume. Hague returned to coach Fesler, who was now enraged.

"Get in there and try for the field goal," he shouted. "Krall and Hamilton out, Hague and Widdoes in!"

By this time, Ohio State had taken too much time. The referee picked up the football and marched off a 5-yard penalty for delay of the game. He placed the ball down on the California 11-yard line, on the hash mark 20 yards in from the sidelines. Now it would be foolish to try for the touchdown.

When Hague finally got into the huddle, Krall and Hamilton, now smiling, trotted off the field.

"What's the big idea?" Hague demanded in the huddle. "Coach Fesler almost had a fit. Why'd you cross him up?"

"We didn't cross him, Jim," said fullback Fred "Curly" Morrison. "We were trying to get you a better kicking angle."

Morrison pointed out that if the play had started on the 6-yard line, the kicking angle would be bad. The five-yard penalty made the kick longer, but improved the angle. The Ohio State players had disobeyed the coach in order to get a penalty!

Holder Widdoes knelt at the California 18-yard line. The ball came back and he placed it down. Hague stepped forward and kicked. The ball just made it over the crossbar. The kick was good, and Ohio State won, 17–14.

There is no record of coach Fesler's reaction.

ALL AROUND THE TOWN

Golf star Walter Hagen and Australian trick-shot artist Joe Kirkwood were the best of friends. They toured together for many years, and they got along so well because they were two of the zaniest people in the world. No matter where they happened to be, Hagen and Kirkwood always had a lot of fun, but they saved their strangest stunts for New York City.

Once they stayed in a hotel that overlooked Central Park. They amused themselves by hitting golf balls out of their hotel window. As far as they knew, they never hit any of the strollers in the park.

Then one day they had an inspiration and decided to make New York City itself a golf course.

To play their crazy round of golf they went a few streets away from their hotel and teed up. They played through the streets, into the hotel lobby, into the elevator, down the corridor of their floor and into their room. Then they went for the "cup" —the toilet bowl.

That was where Hagen always lost the match. Kirkwood could always chip the ball into the toilet bowl but Hagen had difficulty. He always said it was the one shot he could never master.

BATTLE of the SEXES

Bobby Riggs had won the biggest championship in tennis at Wimbledon, England, in 1939. But by 1973, he was 55 years old and more famous for challenging opponents to all sorts of weird matches.

"I'll play you with a poodle tied to each of my legs," he offered one opponent. He also played matches while wearing galoshes, sitting on a chair, and bundled up in a heavy overcoat. Whatever the handicap, Riggs usually won.

The real fuss started when Riggs declared that women couldn't play tennis very well. "They look very pretty in their shorts or miniskirts," he declared, "but they're really not much good. I can beat any woman player even now."

The challenge was taken up by Margaret Court, a 30-year-old Australian who had won six American championships and three at Wimbledon. She was one of the two or three best women players in the world. Court and Riggs agreed to meet on May 13, 1973—Mother's Day—at the San Vicente Country Club in Ramona, California. A prize of $10,000 would go to the winner and nothing to the loser (although the two would share the fees for broadcasting).

It promised to be a good match. Riggs had lost the steam in his service, but he played a very clever game. Court was steady and quick, and she was 25 years younger than her opponent. Before the match, Riggs kept emphasizing the importance of the match and seemed confident of victory. Then, just before the players went on the court, he presented Court with a beautiful bouquet of roses.

When the game began, Court seemed nervous and unsure of herself. Surprisingly, Riggs proceeded to run her off the court, winning in straight sets, 6–2, 6–1. Afterwards, the newspapers called it "The Mother's Day Massacre."

After Court's defeat, Riggs's challenge was taken up by Billie Jean King, who had won five Wimbledon titles. "She plays pretty good for a girl," Riggs grinned. "But I can beat her. I can beat any woman."

Angered, Billie Jean retorted, "Bobby Riggs is a male chauvinist pig, and I'm going to teach him a lesson he'll never forget."

"Aha," Riggs smiled, "We shall see who is the better player. Why, if she beats me, I'll jump off a bridge."

This time the purse was $100,000, and the match was staged at the Astrodome in Houston, Texas. Both Riggs and King also received a lot of extra money from promotion fees and endorsements. Riggs kept interest alive by giving numerous interviews, all the while swallowing vitamin pills by the handful. The match was televised all over the United States, and to 36 other countries via satellite. Riggs was the favorite to win.

For the 30,000 fans at the Astrodome, the event was more like a circus than a tennis match. Billie Jean was brought to courtside on a gold litter carried by four husky members of the Rice University track team. Bobby Riggs made his entrance in a rickshaw with gold wheels pulled by six beautiful girls. The band played stirring marching music.

Bobby Riggs should have picked on someone other than Billie Jean King. She toyed with him, running Riggs all over the court until he was almost ready to drop from exhaustion. When it was done, Billie Jean had won in three straight sets, 6–4, 6–3, 6–3.

Bobby Riggs had failed to prove that an old man could beat a talented young woman in tennis. But his boasting had led to one of the strangest sporting events in history.

HIGH DIVER

Ray Woods played football fairly well, but he was too light to be a star. He wasn't bad at baseball, but not a major leaguer. Still, he wanted to be an athlete.

One day Woods was getting some exercise in a local pool, practicing dives off a board. His form wasn't very good, because Woods tried to leap up as high as he could, and paid no attention to how he hit the water.

"Ray," a friend who was watching said to him, "you're doing it all wrong. It doesn't matter how high you jump. Try to concentrate on hitting the water cleanly."

"Who said height doesn't matter?" Woods retorted. He reminded his friend that an old-timer named Steve Brodie had become famous by jumping off the Brooklyn Bridge. His friend turned away in disgust. But Woods began to think about Steve Brodie. Perhaps he too could make a name for himself by jumping into the water from high places.

Without fanfare, Woods went to New York City. He

16

reached the Brooklyn Bridge, climbed up over the railing, and while onlookers gasped, he jumped. Not only was he uninjured, but Woods did not even need a boat to fish him out of the river.

Overnight he became famous. State fairs all over the United States invited him to make high dives from an assortment of towers. Woods became a great attraction, and in all he made 184 jumps. Only once did he have an accident, but he wasn't seriously hurt.

Then Woods decided to leap from the Oakland Bay Bridge in San Francisco. The authorities did their best to stop him, but he managed to make the jump. It turned out badly. Perhaps he misjudged the height or was caught by the air currents. Whatever the reason, Woods kept flipping over, and he landed on his back. He lived to tell the tale, but he spent two years with straps around his body to heal the broken bones in his back. Two years after the accident he returned to jumping.

Then on April 10, 1942, Ray Woods had his last bit of bad luck. While fishing from a rowboat in the St. Johns River in Florida, he noticed that his line was tangled. He leaned over to yank the line free and lost his balance. Woods fell into the river and drowned.

How strange that a man who had survived jumps of hundreds of feet into the water, should die after falling just a few inches over the side of a rowboat!

Scoring a goal in hockey is usually a big moment for a player. But a Detroit player named Leo Labine once scored a goal he would rather have forgotten.

Montreal was leading Detroit by one goal with seconds left to play. Montreal was playing a man short and there was a face-off in Montreal's zone. The Red Wings pulled their goalie, so that they could mount a six-man power play against Montreal's five defenders. It seemed a great chance to score.

At the face-off, Labine won the draw. He shot a pass toward his point man, who was stationed at the blue line. But the pass went awry, and the puck slid all the way down the ice, 180 feet into the unprotected Detroit net! Labine was credited with a goal—against his own team.

Aiding the Enemy

Sammy Snead and Jimmy Hines competed against each other many times in various golf tournaments. Sometimes Hines beat Snead, sometimes Snead beat Hines. But on one occasion, Jimmy Hines *helped* Snead defeat him.

It happened during the semi-finals of the PGA tournament at Shawnee-on-Delaware, in 1938. On the par-3 thirteenth hole, Snead was inches from the cup after his second shot. Hines was farther away after his first drive. Hines chipped up perfectly—in fact too perfectly. His ball hit Snead's and *both balls* rolled into the cup! Snead hadn't hit his ball, so he could not be charged with a stroke. Both golfers were credited with a birdie 2.

That turned out to be the deciding number. Snead beat Hines by exactly one stroke!

STOP!

All coaches demand obedience from their players. All orders are to be followed. Coach Earl "Red" Blaik of Army always maintained strict discipline.

In one game Army was running up the score against an inexperienced opponent. Blaik did not believe in humiliating a team. So he sent in his third squad with orders to take it easy.

But the opposition could do nothing right that day. Soon one of its players fumbled. A West Point guard scooped up the loose ball and ran toward the goal unopposed. Suddenly he remembered coach Blaik's orders. He stopped in his tracks, looked fearfully at Blaik standing near the bench, and set the ball on the 1-yard line.

STALEMATE

Modern professional wrestling is more of a show-business attraction than a sport. But it wasn't always that way. Many years ago pro wrestlers really competed. In those early matches a wrestler had to pin his man to win.

Ed "Strangler" Lewis was one of the greatest wrestlers of all time. His best hold was a tough-to-break headlock. Equally great was Joe Stecher. When he clamped on a leg-scissors, his opponent began to hurt.

In 1916, these giants of the mat met in the ring at the Omaha Fair Grounds. The match started at four o'clock in the afternoon under a hot sun. For the first hour neither of them went down, but they locked hands and shoved, pushed, pulled and grunted. Then they began flying all over the ring, throwing each other around like sacks of potatoes.

It grew dark and a few cars were driven up to ringside and their lights turned on. On and on they struggled. Finally, at nine o'clock, after five hours of tremendous effort, the match was called a draw.

Strangely enough, a couple of years earlier, these same two wrestlers had slammed at each other for two hours, and the match was called a draw. And a couple of years after their five-hour match, they went at it again, also for two hours. Once more the match ended in a draw.

DOUBLE TROUBLE

One of the most difficult issues in sports is deciding who is an amateur and who is a professional. The team from Berlin (later renamed Kitchener), Ontario, found this out, much to its sorrow.

In the early 1900s, the Berlin team was the best club in the Ontario Hockey Association, a senior amateur league. Hockey was as rough then as it is today, and one season a player named Jimmy McGinnis suffered several fractured ribs. Since he was an amateur, McGinnis had a paying job, other than hockey. But when he was injured, he couldn't work. The Berlin team generously agreed to pay his wages of $25 a week until he recovered.

Much later, at the end of the season, Berlin won the Western section of the Senior Series, and met the Toronto St. Georges in the series finals. Berlin won the first game, 6–1, on St. George's ice, and seemed certain to repeat in the next game.

At this point, the story of Jimmy McGinnis leaked out. He had received $50 to cover the loss of his wages while he was in the hospital. But this was amateur hockey. No one was supposed to be paid. St. George protested to the league officials, claiming that McGinnis was now a professional. The Ontario Hockey Association upheld the protest and ruled that Berlin had to drop McGinnis from the team and replay the first game of the final series, which Berlin had won so easily.

The Berlin team went on strike. Team members flatly refused to play that game all over again. So, in front of a large home crowd, the St. George center faced off against himself.

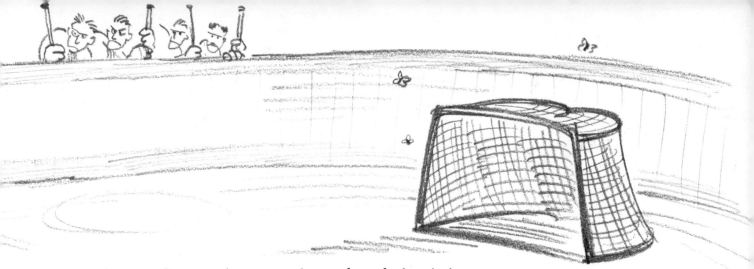

Another St. George player got the puck and shot it into an empty net. The Berlin players watched angrily from the bench. The referee stopped the game and awarded St. George the game by the score of 9–0. Nobody on the Berlin team had even made a move.

The fans were not very happy over this turn of events. They wanted some hockey. Something had to be done quickly. The teams had a brief conference, and agreed to play against each other for a purse of $100. It would be an exhibition game, nothing more. The charged-up Berlin team proceeded to beat St. George soundly.

Now the officials of the Ontario Hockey Association stepped in again. This time they decided the $100 purse had made the whole Berlin team professional. Unless the money was returned, the team would be disqualified from amateur hockey. If they refused, the Berlin Intermediates, a sister team, would also be suspended.

The money was returned. But because of their sit-down strike, the Berlin seniors lost the Senior Series. They had lost because the team was generous enough to pay an injured player. And they almost got thrown out of the league because they beat the team that had won the series without opposition.

In 1968, Tommy Moore of Hagerstown, Maryland, became the youngest golf player ever to score a hole-in-one. It happened on the 145-yard fourth hole at Woodbrier Golf Course in Martinsburg, West Virginia. At the time Tommy was exactly six years, one month, one week old.

Later in the year he did it again!

60-SECOND DISASTER

When Ohio State and Notre Dame met to play football in 1935, both teams were undefeated. The teams were evenly matched, and the game was one of the most exciting ever played. But for some strange reason the outcome seemed to depend on a reserve halfback for Ohio State named Dick Beltz.

Ohio State took control at first. It scored two straight touchdowns and led, 13–0. Dick Beltz was the kicker who scored one of the extra points.

Finally Notre Dame scored a touchdown, but missed the point-after. The score was 13–6. Then late in the fourth period Notre Dame got another touchdown. But once more the kick failed, so Ohio State led, 13–12.

With about a minute to play Ohio State had the ball. The extra point made by Dick Beltz was the difference between the two teams. All Ohio State had to do was hold onto the ball until the clock ran out. Undoubtedly, Beltz would be the big hero.

But the game had run only 59 minutes. A lot could happen in that final minute—both to Ohio State and to Dick Beltz.

First, Beltz got the assignment of carrying the ball for the Buckeyes. He tried an end sweep. Half of the Notre Dame line helped stop him, and they knocked the ball from his hands. Notre Dame recovered. Suddenly it had one last chance to win the game.

On the first play Andy Pilney of Notre Dame ran the ball down to the Ohio State 19. But he was hit so hard he had to be taken off the field on a stretcher. He was replaced by a player with the unlikely name William Shakespeare.

Shakespeare tried a pass, but he threw the ball badly—right at Dick Beltz. (Players in the 1930s played both offense and defense.) No player from Notre Dame was within five yards of him. All he had to do to assure a victory for Ohio State was catch the ball.

He dropped it!

Again Notre Dame tried a last-ditch pass. It was thrown to Wayne Milner, a sure-handed receiver. Milner caught the ball, and only one Ohio State player had a chance to stop the score—Dick Beltz. He lunged at Milner, but missed. The Irish of Notre Dame scored, and moments later the game was over. Final score: Notre Dame 18, Ohio State 13.

There wasn't a more dejected football player in the United States than Dick Beltz. With one minute left he had been the hero of the game, because his conversion had given Ohio State a one-point edge. But then 1) his fumble gave Notre Dame possession of the football; 2) his failure to make an easy interception gave Notre Dame still another chance; and 3) the winning pass had been thrown over his head.

It had all happened within a period of 60 seconds. In that one minute, Dick Beltz had changed from a hero to a goat.

ONE–MAN SHOW

Basketball is a team game. Individual stars are helpful, but in the end, the team that plays together is the team that wins. No one player can hog the ball; no one player should do all the shooting. Every player, every coach and every fan knows that. But once in a while, a team needs a super effort by an individual. In a National Basketball Association playoff game between Boston and Syracuse, Boston's Bob Cousy made one of the most spectacular one-man shows ever seen.

The Boston Celtics were losing by two points with only two seconds left to play. Then Bob Cousy was fouled. Calmly, he sent both free throws through the hoop to tie the game and send it into overtime.

Once again Syracuse took the lead. With seconds left and Syracuse ahead, Cousy was fouled. He made the shot good. The game went into a second overtime.

Doggedly, Syracuse went ahead again. With only a few ticks left on the clock, Cousy took a pass, drove in and scored his lay-up to tie the game, making a third overtime necessary.

By then the crowd was going crazy with excitement. Boston's publicity director, Howard McHugh, fainted. But in the third overtime Syracuse opened a commanding lead and led by five points with just 13 seconds to go. The game seemed over. But Cousy drove to the basket again, made his shot good and drew a foul. He sank the free throw to cut the margin to two points. With only 5 seconds remaining, the Celtics got the ball back and threw it to Cousy. Near midcourt, he let fly a long one-hander just as the buzzer sounded. The ball went in. Tie score. Fourth overtime.

It took only two and a half minutes for Syracuse to build up another five-point lead. However, Cousy went on the war-

path again. He hit a shot from outside, then drove in for a lay-up, and made a foul shot. Boston took the lead and held it to the end. Final score, 111–105, Boston.

In that game Bob Cousy scored a total of 50 points. He made 25 of them in regulation time, and 25 more in the four overtime periods. And he made 30 out of 32 foul shots. Even more important, he had scored his points at the right time. Four times he scored in the final seconds to keep the game going. Then he helped his team pull away.

Basketball may be a team game, but most teams would not be sorry to have an individual performer like Bob Cousy.

Five-Dollar Putter

In July 1964, golfer Bobby Nichols went to a party at Owl Creek Country Club near his hometown, Louisville, Kentucky. Feeling restless because he was going to play in the PGA the following week, Nichols wandered into the pro shop and began to poke around the items offered for sale. He found a used putter that struck his fancy.

"How much?" Nichols asked.

"Five dollars."

"I'll take it."

In the PGA tournament at the Columbus Country Club in Ohio, the putter began to earn back its purchase price. In the first round Nichols carded a 64, scoring eight birdies. Four times he dropped the ball in from more than ten feet out.

In the third round the putter saved Nichols from disaster. He should have been way over par; instead, he shot a 69. Nichols made good a 10-footer on the first hole, a 20-footer on the second hole, a 15-footer on the twelfth and a 25-footer on the fifteenth.

The magic putter continued to serve him well in the fourth round. On the tenth hole he popped a beautiful 35-foot putt for an eagle. On the fifteenth, he made good a 15-foot tap, followed by one from 12 feet out on the sixteenth. But the putt that brought gasps from the crowd was the one on the seventeenth hole. From just over 50 feet away, Nichols rolled the ball into the cup. His putting had made him the PGA champ.

Incredibly, Bobby Nichols had made only 119 putts for the total of 72 holes. Even the great Jack Nicklaus had made 134 putts in the tournament. Nichols gave all the credit to the old putter he had picked up in a pro shop for five dollars.

The Dullest Game

The best professional basketball team of the early 1950s was the Minneapolis Lakers. They made scoring look easy, particularly when their star center, 6-foot-10 George Mikan, was in the game. There was only one way to keep them from running up a lot of points, and that was to stall. (The 24-second clock had not been invented.) Opponents tried to freeze the ball by passing it around, dribbling—anything to keep control of the ball.

Such strategy didn't work very often because the Lakers usually jumped into the lead, forcing the other team to take more shots. Big Mikan was always there to snatch the rebound. But once it did work. As a result of that game professional basketball changed drastically.

On November 22, 1950, the Lakers played against the Fort Wayne Pistons in Minneapolis. The Pistons went into their "slow motion" tactics immediately.

The fans didn't like what was happening, and they began to boo, whistle and stomp. The Pistons turned a deaf ear. The referee couldn't do anything, because the Pistons' tactics were legal at that time. At the end of the first period Fort Wayne was ahead, 8–7.

Nothing much happened in the second period either. The Lakers rang up six points, the Pistons added only three, and at half time Minneapolis was ahead, 13–11.

There wasn't a great deal of difference in the third period. Minneapolis scored four,

Fort Wayne tallied five, and at the end of the quarter the scoreboard read 17–16, Minneapolis.

The final period was incredible! It seemed that all the players on the court had fallen asleep. Then, with nine seconds to go and the Lakers leading, 18–17, Larry Foust of Fort Wayne drove in and scored the go-ahead points. Little Slater Martin of the Lakers tried to win the game with a desperation shot, but failed. Fort Wayne won the game, 19–18.

Without doubt it was the dullest game in the history of the National Basketball Association. Of course, several records were set, but they were the wrong kind of records:

- Fewest shots at the basket, both teams.
- Fewest points scored in a quarter.
- Fewest points scored in a half.
- Fewest points scored in a game.

George Mikan was the only Laker to score from the floor; he tossed in four baskets. He also made good on seven free throws, meaning that he scored 15 of his team's 18 points.

Fans, sportswriters and league officials were very angry. Maurice Podoloff, president of the NBA, declared, "It'll never happen again!"

Soon afterward, the pros adopted the 24-second rule, which forces a team to shoot within 24 seconds or give up the ball. At least something good came out of basketball's dullest game.

SELF-DESTRUCTION

Heavyweight boxer Jack Doyle was nicknamed "The Irish Thrush." He was handsome, and he liked to sing Irish songs. However, other boxers didn't think much of his fighting ability. After his "bout" with a fighter named Eddie Phillips, it became clear that Doyle would never threaten any champions.

In the second round, Doyle advanced on Phillips and threw a mighty roundhouse right. He missed completely. Doyle's momentum carried him over the ropes. He hit his head on the ring apron, knocking himself unconscious, and fell to the floor below. The referee counted ten and the fight was over.

Jack Doyle had succeeded in knocking himself out!

Committee No-Hittee

Usually when a pitcher has his stuff and is getting the other team out, the manager leaves him in the game. He hopes the pitcher can stay in for nine innings so that the relief pitchers can be rested for another day.

When the Oakland Athletics faced the California Angels at the end of the 1975 season, however, starting pitcher Vida Blue knew he would pitch only five innings.

The Athletics had already clinched a spot in the American League playoffs. Manager Alvin Dark wanted Blue to get a workout, but at the same time he didn't want the ace left-hander to get too tired. Five innings seemed just about right.

Blue's fastball was humming and his slider was breaking over the corners. Only three batters reached base against him, two on walks and one on an error by shortstop Bert Campaneris.

Relief pitcher Glen Abbott also needed a workout, and he pitched the sixth inning. He set the Angels down in one-two-three order.

Paul Lindblad pitched the seventh inning for the Athletics. He faced three batters and retired them all. Finally, Rollie Fingers mopped up in the eighth and ninth. Nobody got on base against him.

It was the first time four pitchers had ever combined to pitch a no-hit game. Only twice before had two pitchers gotten together on a no-hitter, and both of these occasions were strange for other reasons.

In 1917, Babe Ruth started a game for the Boston Red Sox. He pitched to one batter and walked him. But Ruth was angry at the umpire's calls. He complained so bitterly that he was thrown out of the game. Ernie Shore came in to pitch. The base runner was thrown out trying to steal second. Then Shore retired every single batter in order, pitching a perfect game!

The other combined no-hitter happened in 1967. Steve Barber and Stu Miller of the Baltimore Orioles teamed up to blank the other side in the hit column. But an unearned run scored and the Orioles lost the game.

Football players hate cold weather. Their hands are raw, and every contact with an opponent makes their bodies ache. One player found a way to avoid the cold.

In 1932 Loyola of the South went north to play Butler College in Indianapolis, Indiana. It was so cold that fans were warming their hands over small kerosene stoves. Huge bales of hay were piled along the sidelines near the benches.

Loyola end Mal Simmons almost froze during the first half. Just before the second half opened, Simmons hid inside one of the bales of hay and stayed there, snug and warm. Coach Clark Shaughnessy shouted himself hoarse calling for Simmons. At the end of the game Simmons sneaked out of the hay and ran into the dressing room. He told coach Shaughnessy he hadn't heard him call because he had his hands over his ears to keep them warm.

TRICK SHOTS

In all sports, fans enjoy seeing players do tricks. For example, the Harlem Globetrotters entertain basketball fans by drop-kicking "field goals" through the hoop and by bouncing the ball off their heads, their feet and other parts of their anatomy. Also in basketball, a man named Wilfred Hetzel made a career out of shooting through the hoop while on his knees, or with his back turned to the basket, or while keeping his eyes shut.

But some of the greatest trick-shot specialists were golfers. What they could do was almost unbelievable.

Joe Kirkwood, an Australian golfer, could swing *backwards* and drive the ball out of a sand trap right near the cup. He played right-handed with left-handed clubs and vice versa. He could pop the ball high into the air and catch it without moving from his tracks. And he could tee up two balls and hit them at the same time, causing one to hook and the other to slice.

Another trick-shot specialist, Paul Hahn, could also do the hook-slice trick, and a few others, too, that he invented. He boomed out shots while on his knees, or while standing with one foot on a chair. He could hit the ball two hundred yards with a clubhead attached to a length of garden hose.

Hahn had one trick which caused some trouble. He used a beautiful girl; she lay flat on the ground with a golf ball resting on her lips. Hahn swung and hit the ball without touching the girl. But he soon had to give up showing that trick, when he found out that some youngsters were trying to copy the trick using their own girl friends.

Among modern golfers, the trick-shot prize probably belongs to Lee Trevino. Before he became well known by winning major tournaments, he made a living by placing bets with amateur golfers that he could beat them even under the strangest handicaps. He once beat a golfer who used regulation clubs while he played with *only* a soda bottle!

SPEED DEMONS

Bonneville Salt Flats in Utah is the dried bed of an ancient lake. Its climate is almost unbearable. In winter, heavy rains flood the flats, creating deep ponds. In summer, the sun beats down mercilessly, drying up much of the water and leaving a blinding white stretch of salt. The twelve-mile stretch of hard salt has only one use: it is the "course" used for attempts to break the world land speed record.

In a way, this is not really an automobile race, since cars do not compete against each other. They race against the clock. A car gets off to a flying start, and then it speeds through a measured mile in one direction. Then the car does the same thing in the opposite direction. Both times are averaged out, and the result is recorded by officials of the United States Auto Club.

Three monster cars came to Bonneville in 1964 to make a run at the world's record. Walt Arfons owned the "Wingfoot Express," which was 24 feet long, weighed 4,800 pounds, and was sponsored by Goodyear. His brother, Art Arfons, had a 21-foot racer that weighed 6,000 pounds and was sponsored by Firestone. The car was named "Green Monster." Craig Breedlove was the third man. His car, "Spirit of America," was sponsored by Goodyear and Shell. It was 34 feet long and weighed 8,000 pounds.

The only one of the three who would not drive over the course was Walt Arfons. He had been ill, and his partner, Tom Green, was at the wheel.

Tom Green made his run on October 2, 1964. He zoomed

over the salt flats at 406 miles per hour one way, and 420 miles per hour coming back, for an average of 413 miles per hour. It was a new record.

The record lasted exactly three days. Art Arfons streaked 396 mph, and then 479 mph, for an average of 434 mph. As he finished the run a tire blew, and the car's rear end was damaged. But it came to a stop safely.

Art Arfons's record did not hold up either. Eight days later, Craig Breedlove hurtled over the course at an average speed of 468.719 mph. In eleven days three new records had been set. But there was still more to come. Tom Green had gone as fast as his car would go. But Breedlove and Art Arfons knew their cars could go still faster.

Breedlove gave it another try, and for the fourth consecutive time another record was set, this time 525 mph. Then the car began to swerve. Breedlove pressed the parachute button, and the twin chutes popped out behind the car, but they were ripped loose. He went out of control at 500 miles an hour, heading straight for a telephone pole. Breedlove expected the car to flip over, but miraculously it didn't. His axle cut through the pole like a hot knife through butter, and then the car went up over a hill and nose down into a brine pond. Breedlove freed himself from the car and swam to shore. Jittery, thankful to escape with his life, Breedlove joked, "For my next act I will set myself on fire."

A couple of weeks later it was Art Arfons's turn to break

the record. He knew that Breedlove's car could not run again until it was repaired. Arfons gunned his "Green Monster" to a two-way average of 536.71, and the record was his again.

The five heats had produced five straight new records! Now the rainy season came and there was no more racing at Bonneville that year.

In 1965 Art Arfons and Craig Breedlove were at it again. On November 2, Breedlove, with a repaired and improved car, fairly flew over the course at 555.127 mph, and he had the record again.

Art Arfons was not to be denied. He wanted that record and he got it, at an average speed of 576.553. As he was trying to slow down the car swerved and hit a surveyor's post in the ground that somebody had forgotten to remove. The front end of the "Green Monster" was smashed and the tire flew off. The car veered and swerved and careened as smoke and fumes enveloped it. Somehow Arfons brought the car to a stop and jumped out. The "Green Monster" was a mess, but Art Arfons had his record. It was the seventh consecutive time the world land speed record had been broken.

Now only Breedlove was left. Art Arfons would not be able to challenge any more, at least not that year. On November 15, Breedlove bulleted his car 593.178 mph one way, and then, like a guided missile, he tore over the course at 608.201 mph coming back. His average was 600.601. Craig Breedlove became the first man ever to drive a car through the 600-mph barrier!

And between them, Breedlove, Arfons and Tom Green had broken the record eight times in eight successive starts!

For Craig Breedlove, there was only one more world to conquer. He asked his wife if she would drive his car and try to set a new women's speed record, which was then 270 miles per hour. Although she had never driven a car in competition, Mrs. Breedlove agreed. It wasn't hard, as she found out. She drove her husband's car an average of 307 mph to set a new record.

The Breedloves were the fastest-driving couple in the world.

Bumper Crop

One of baseball's greatest pitchers was an Indian named Albert "Chief" Bender, who pitched for the Philadelphia Athletics and Phillies. Bender won 208 games in the majors, but his own favorite story concerned a game he lost as a bush-leaguer.

In 1901 Bender agreed to pitch his first professional game for the Dillsburg, Pennsylvania, team. He was to be paid five dollars. Even Bender had to laugh when he saw where the game would be played. It was a hayfield, with a cabbage patch in the outfield. Bender himself hit a home run into the cabbage patch, but he lost the game in the tenth inning.

Afterward, the manager handed the Chief $3.20. "We don't have enough money," the manager explained. "I'll give you the rest the next time I see you."

After 41 years, the Chief was interviewed by Ed Pollock, a reporter for the *Philadelphia Bulletin.* As he was recalling his early years in baseball, Bender told the story of the Dillsburg game, and Pollock included it in his story.

A few days later, a letter and a small canvas bag reached the *Bulletin.* They were addressed to Chief Bender, in care of the *Bulletin.* The letter read, in part:

> Dear Sir:
> In going over our records we have an outstanding account due you from the summer of 1901. . . .
> Not knowing your whereabouts nor having seen you for all these years, we were unable to remit. The cabbages were harvested and sold later that year, giving us a little surplus. We are enclosing the money reserved for you. . . .
> Yours truly,
> Dillsburg Baseball Club
> Dillsburg, Pa.

In the canvas bag were a three-cent piece with the date 1864, a two-cent piece, two dimes dated 1875, 23 nickels and

40 Indian-head pennies. The change added up to $1.80, the exact amount Bender was owed. But the Dillsburg team was really being generous. The coins were very rare and worth a great deal more than their face value.

OVERTIMES

Nothing is particularly strange about a basketball game that goes into overtime. It happens all the time. Two overtime periods is by no means extraordinary. Three overtime stanzas is uncommon, and four is pretty rare. But after that the overtime periods usually stop. In fact, in the history of basketball, only four games have gone into a sixth overtime. All were played by college teams.

On February 21, 1953, Niagara and Siena were tied at 54–all at the end of regulation play. Then the overtime periods began, and it seemed that they would never end. In the first overtime both teams scored seven points; in the second, two points; in the third, seven again; in the fourth, two again; in the fifth, five points. Tired? So were the players. At last, Niagara spurted ahead to stay in the sixth extra frame, and won by a score of 88–81. Eddie Fleming of Niagara played the entire 70 minutes of basketball, and thereafter his number was changed to 70.

Two years later, Western Illinois University played St. Ambrose College. With four seconds to play, Western Illinois scored the tying basket to make the score 51–51.

After that came the usual freeze, the pass-around and the stalling, with each team waiting to try the last-second shot to win the game. In the six overtimes the two teams scored only 13 points. Finally, Western Illinois made a last-second shot in the sixth overtime and won, 58–57.

The only major college game with six overtimes occurred in 1955 between Purdue and Minnesota. Each team had 57 points when the clock ran out. After four overtimes —another full half of basketball—the score was exactly the same! Not one point had been scored. Each team scored two points in the fifth overtime. Then they gave up their stalling tactics. Minnesota outscored Purdue ten to seven in the final period to win, 69–66.

On January 5, 1957, Coe College and Monmouth College tangled in still another marathon game. Each team scored two points in each of the first five overtimes. Finally, Coe scored three points to none in overtime six, and won, 65–62.

Since 1957 no six-overtime games have been reported. But sooner or later some teams somewhere will deadlock again. Seven overtimes, anyone?

NUMBER 9

In certain sports, the great stars seem to wear a particular number on their jerseys. For example, in football, number 32 was worn by Jim Brown and O.J. Simpson. They were the two greatest running backs in football history.

In hockey, the "star number" is 9.

The fabulous Charlie Conacher, who was part of Toronto's great "Kid Line" back in the 1930s wore that number, and so did some other hockey greats. But the tradition really started with Maurice "Rocket" Richard of the Montreal Canadiens, who was as famous in hockey as Babe Ruth in baseball.

Richard wore number 15 until his son was born. Because his son weighed nine pounds at birth, the Rocket asked for, and received, number 9 to wear.

There was a time when lower berths on trains were assigned to players who had been with the team for a long time, or had low numbers on their sweaters. Gordie Howe had been wearing number 17, but when number 9 opened up because of a trade, he asked for it. He may have wanted the same number as Richard, but more likely he just wanted a better night's sleep when the team was traveling by train.

Bobby Hull had two different numbers, 16 and 7. Gordie Howe had always been his idol, and finally Bobby asked for number 9 for his own sweater. Thus, he kept this unofficial tradition alive. And three of hockey's all-time great players all wore the number 9.

Mudbath Heroes

Two of the greatest college football players of the 1930s were Gaynell Tinsley and Sammy Baugh. Tinsley, who played for Louisiana State University, was one of the best pass receivers ever to play the game. Baugh, from Texas Christian University, was a great passer who later became an all-pro passer for the Washington Redskins.

On January 1, 1936, Louisiana State and Texas Christian met in the Sugar Bowl. All the experts figured that Baugh would star with his passing, and Tinsley would catch his share of passes. Both players did star in the game, but not the way the experts thought.

It had begun to rain the day before the game, and it was still raining when the teams began to play. The field looked like a big mudbath. It was not a good day for throwing or receiving passes.

In the second period, Louisiana State made the first serious threat of the day. It had the ball inside the Texas Christian 10-yard line. But four plays into the line fell short. So Baugh's Texas team took over on downs on its own 2-yard line.

During the 1930s players played all 60 minutes of the game—there were no offensive or defensive specialists. So when Louisiana State lost the ball, Gaynell Tinsley became a defensive end.

Texas Christian lined up in short punt formation. Baugh was far back in his end zone to do the kicking. Tinsley saw an opportunity to block the punt. But Baugh was planning to cross up the defense by throwing a quick pass instead. As Baugh drew back his arm to pass, Tinsley was after him. The end chased the passer all over the muddy end zone. The wet ball squirted out of Baugh's hand and bounced out of the end zone.

Tinsley had forced a safety, so his team led, 2–0.

Early in the third quarter, Texas Christian recovered a fumble on the Louisiana 40-yard line. Once again Baugh decided to gamble on a pass—but not on his own. He took the snap from center and handed off to halfback Jimmy Lawrence. Lawrence threw to end Will Walls, and the play carried to the LSU 17-yard line.

Three running plays didn't gain much ground. So Baugh called for a field goal. He placed the ball on the 26 and TCU kicker Talden "Tilly" Manton kicked it over the crossbar. TCU led, 3–2.

The game settled down to a muddy duel. Tinsley played a great defensive game. And Baugh's booming punts kept Louisiana State pinned in its own territory. He punted 14 times that day, averaging 44.6 yards per punt. In the third quarter, playing defense, Baugh intercepted two passes deep in his own territory. Near the end of the game, he broke loose on a 44-yard run, carrying the ball to the Louisiana 2-yard line. But Louisiana put up a tough goal-line stand, and in four running plays Texas *lost* 9 yards.

The final score was 3–2, and the game came to be known as "the football game with the baseball score."

Oddly enough, Gaynell Tinsley, one of the best pass catchers in the nation, did very little receiving. But he was probably the best defensive player on the Louisiana State team that day. It was Tinsley who forced the fumble that caused LSU to score its only points of the day.

And Sammy Baugh, considered the best passer in college football, did almost no passing, but his defensive play and his running took Texas Christian to victory.

Who's That Runner?

Some of the best distance runners of the South came to Birmingham, Alabama, in 1941 to compete in the Southern Collegiate Conference meet. One of the events of the day was the two-mile run. It would be a grueling race, for the day was hot, and the eight quarter-mile laps seemed endless.

The runners took off at the sound of the gun, and settled down for the long run. Then one of the runners took the lead. Spectators and officials checked their records. That boy wasn't supposed to be in the race at all.

Referee C. W. Streit thought he recognized the runner. It was Walter Spain, a boy from a nearby high school. Moving onto the track, the referee tried to grab Spain's arm as he went by, but the youngster dodged and kept on running.

On the next lap a group of policemen were waiting for Spain and they forced him to the sidelines. Referee Streit began to give Spain a stern lecture. But suddenly the young runner broke away, and the crowd was up and roaring. Spain wasn't running from the police; he wanted to get back into the race. The police started to chase him again, but Streit called out, "No, let him run. If he wants to race that badly, leave him alone."

Spain had lost half a lap because of the police, but he sprinted madly after the pack. Soon he was even with the last runner, and then moved by. Pounding into the home stretch Spain kept passing the runners, as the crowd cheered him on. He reached fourth position, but that was as far as the high school runner could go. He dropped back to fifth, and that was where he finished —unofficially.

As a rule, golf tournaments are not played in the rain. But one year, during the Southern California Women's Open, the golfers were caught in a downpour. Mary K. Brown was drenched as she tried to putt out on the last hole. But the cup was full of water. The ball rolled across the water and kept going, over the cup and down the hill, caught in a little rivulet of water. Luckily the officials saw what happened. When the rain stopped they let her take the stroke over.

LIGHTNING STRIKES TWICE

Among the great moments in baseball, the 1951 playoff series between the Brooklyn Dodgers and the New York Giants is near the top of the list. The last game of that series was probably the most dramatic in the history of the game.

The two teams were tied at the end of the regular season, so a three-game playoff series was scheduled to decide which team would go on to the World Series. The Giants won the first game, 3–1. The Dodgers won the second, 10–0. In the deciding game, the Giants were behind, 4–1, when they came to bat in the ninth inning. They scored one run and had two men on base with one out when Bobby Thomson came up. He hit a home run to win the game and the playoffs for the Giants. Sportswriters called the homer "The shot heard round the world."

Kneeling in the on-deck circle was a great young rookie named Willie Mays. Later, reporters asked Mays what he would have done if Thomson had not hit the homer, and the responsibility for winning the game had fallen on his shoulders.

"I don't know," Mays replied honestly. "I was just a kid then. There was a lot of pressure. Maybe I'd have struck out."

Such a dramatic event seemed unlikely ever to repeat itself, and Willie Mays probably thought he'd never get a second chance to win a pennant with one swing of the bat. But he did. Eleven years later the whole situation repeated itself!

In 1958 the New York Giants moved to San Francisco and the Brooklyn Dodgers moved to Los Angeles.

Then in 1962, eleven years after that memorable playoff series in New York City, the Giants and Dodgers ended the season in a tie for first place. A three-game series was scheduled to determine a pennant-winner.

In the 1951 series, the Giants had won the first playoff game. In 1962, they won the first playoff game.

In the 1951 series, the Dodgers had won the second playoff game. In 1962, they won the second playoff game.

In the 1951 series, the Giants had come into the ninth inning trailing the Dodgers. In 1962, the Giants came into the ninth inning trailing the Dodgers.

This time the Giants loaded the bases in the ninth. Then up came Willie Mays. Eleven years earlier, he might have struck out because of the pressure. Now he had a second chance—a real one.

He hit a drive off the foot of pitcher Ed Roebuck. It went for a single, scoring a run. Orlando Cepeda flied out, but the tying run scored. Then a wild pitch and an error gave the Giants the ball game and the pennant. They won the playoffs just as they had in 1951.

Only one man saw the playoffs from both sides. In 1951, when the Giants won, their manager had been Leo Durocher. In 1962, Durocher learned about losing—he was a coach for the Los Angeles Dodgers.

FIELD-GOAL TENDING

R.C. Owens, a pass receiver for the San Francisco 49ers and Baltimore Colts, had been a marvelous basketball player and high jumper in college. He had once led the nation in rebounds, at 27.7 per game, and he had high-jumped seven feet. Owens's great ability to leap high made him valuable to the 49ers as a receiver, too. With his quarterback, Y.A. Tittle, Owens perfected a play called the Alley-Oop. Tittle would throw a high floating pass, and Owens would outjump the defensive players and catch the ball just as if it were a basketball rebound.

During one game in 1960, against the Detroit Lions, a Detroit field goal attempt barely cleared the crossbar. A teammate said jokingly to Owens, "I'll bet you could've gotten that, R.C."

Owens thought about that for a while. Both the basketball hoop and the football crossbar are ten feet off the ground. Although he was only 6-foot-3, he had blocked many basketball shots. Why couldn't he do the same on a field goal attempt? San Francisco coach Red Hickey wouldn't let him try it, but when Owens was traded to the Colts, coach Weeb Ewbank thought it wasn't such a bad idea.

Owens first got a chance to try out his scheme when the Colts played the Washington Redskins. Bob Khayat of the Redskins attempted a field goal from the Baltimore 40-yard line. Owens waited under the crossbar. He had been practicing his block for a long time to get the timing right. The kick went off. The ball rose, and then as it began to descend, Owens flexed his legs and let go with a mighty leap. His fingers made contact with the ball and tipped it away.

The trick never caught on with other teams, probably because they didn't have a leaper with Owens's strength and timing. So Owens still holds the record for goal tending in football.

The Rally

From the time the Milwaukee Bucks became a new NBA team in 1968–69, the New York Knicks always seemed to be able to beat them. Even when the Bucks signed Lew Alcindor (who later changed his name to Kareem Abdul-Jabbar), nothing seemed to work for them. Although the big center had made the Bucks a winning basketball team, he wasn't enough to beat the Knicks. In the 1970 playoffs, the Knicks eliminated the Bucks by winning four games out of five. In the 1970–71 regular-season schedule, again the Knicks beat Milwaukee four out of five.

In 1972 it seemed that Milwaukee had broken the jinx against the Knicks. Willis Reed, the New York center, had bad legs. Alcindor could operate fairly much as he pleased. And on November 18, 1972, the Bucks were all set to face New York on the Knicks' own home court.

With just under six minutes left to play, Milwaukee was ahead 86–68. With the Knicks down by 18 points, even the

huge crowd of Knick fans was ready to accept the defeat. But the Knicks weren't.

Knick guard Earl Monroe scored a lay-up. In the next few minutes, the Bucks missed their shots and had the ball stolen from them while the New York guards, Monroe and Walt Frazier, scored nine straight points. Then big Dave DeBusschere hit on a long jumper to make the score 86–79. The Knicks were only seven down.

Milwaukee desperately began taking shots, but nothing seemed to work. Monroe and Frazier kept whittling down the lead, and with 47 seconds left, the Knicks were behind by only a single point.

Lucius Allen of Milwaukee had a chance to help the Bucks along when he was fouled. He missed two straight free throws. Walt Frazier grabbed the rebound and zinged a fast pass to Monroe, who scored. Now the Knicks were ahead. The crowd in Madison Square Garden was screaming itself hoarse.

The Knicks got the ball back with 26 seconds left on the clock. They dribbled around, not even taking a shot when they had a chance. Milwaukee got the ball out of bounds with 2 seconds left. But the last-ditch try by Alcindor fell short. The Knicks won, 87–86.

Rallies have won games for many teams, but this one was spectacular. In the last 5 minutes 50 seconds, the Milwaukee Bucks did not score a single point, and the Knicks scored 19, exactly the number they needed to win the game.

INSTANT RECORD

Like all athletes, Bill Mosienko of the Chicago Black Hawks dreamed of getting his name in the record book. On March 23, 1952, he did it—in less time than it will take you to read this story.

The Black Hawks were playing the New York Rangers. During the action, Black Hawk Gus Bodnar got the puck and passed to Mosienko. He flashed in on the net and scored.

At the following face-off, Bodnar gained possession again. He passed to Mosienko, who broke away, skated in, shot and scored.

Once more Bodnar won the face-off at center ice. This time he passed to left-winger George Gee, as Mosienko skated in on the right. Gee flicked the rubber to him, Mosienko shot—and scored.

Bill Mosienko had scored three goals in exactly 21 seconds! It was the fastest hat trick on record.

Asleep at the Wheel

Many experienced racing drivers say that the Le Mans sports car race is the toughest of all. They have many reasons for feeling that way.

First, the race is an endurance test lasting 24 hours. It begins at four o'clock in the afternoon and ends at four o'clock the following afternoon. The winner is the car that has run the most laps.

Second, no one can predict the weather. The race might begin in bright sunshine, only to be replaced by a night fog or heavy rains. Sunrise brings bright glare.

Third, the course is tricky. It runs on city streets and is filled with tricky curves and sharp turns. Because cars often break down, the road becomes dotted with dangerous oil slicks, which are hard to see at night.

For those reasons (and many other reasons as well) each car must have two drivers. One rests for a while, trying to nap, or drink coffee, while his partner is spinning around the course. Then it is his turn to get behind the wheel and drive through the turns, the tunnels, the gritty roads.

But the rule requiring two drivers had not come along in 1952. In that year a Frenchman named Pierre Levegh decided he could drive the whole race by himself without a relief driver.

Levegh drove a Talbot, a good, durable sports car. He had spent long weeks planning exactly how he would drive, and when the race got under way, he stuck to his plan.

Through the long afternoon and night Levegh drove on, stopping only briefly to fuel up, to change a tire, and to drink a quick cup of coffee. By morning he was leading by four laps. Many of the other cars had dropped out of the race.

Racing fans along the route marveled at the daring driver. He wasn't a young man—indeed, Levegh was over 50 years old at the time!—yet he continued to drive mile after grueling mile.

By three o'clock in the afternoon Levegh had a 25-mile lead. Only courage and determination kept him going. But he was almost exhausted, and his brain was getting fuzzy. He could no longer make the split-second decisions that were necessary in order to handle the car.

Going into one curve he tried to shift into a higher gear. But his reflexes were dulled. Instead, he shifted into a lower gear. The car's engine stalled. Levegh could not start it. He was taken off the track, numb, crying uncontrollably.

Pierre Levegh had come within less than an hour of winning the Le Mans endurance race all by himself.

NERVES

Basketball coaches are often nervous. But no coach was more nervous than Joe Lapchick. It's amazing that he didn't quit coaching. But he managed to live with his nerves for more than 30 years as a coach.

In 1944 Lapchick was coaching St. John's University. The Redmen had a great team that got to the finals of the National Invitational Tournament. Then they faced DePaul, sparked by big George Mikan, for the championship. When DePaul pulled into the lead, Lapchick was dying a thousand deaths. Then with five minutes left in the game, Mikan fouled out. St. John's caught up and then passed DePaul. With a minute left, it seemed sure that St. John's would win. Lapchick didn't see the end of the game, however. He had fainted on the bench.

In 1952, coaching the New York Knicks, Lapchick watched as Fort Wayne came from behind, scoring the winning points with only two seconds to play. He walked dazedly into the Knick locker room and collapsed. He was in the hospital for three days.

In another game Lapchick got so angry at the referee that he disgustedly threw a whole water bucket high into the air. The water came down on Lapchick. Luckily, the bucket fell harmlessly to the floor.

But perhaps Lapchick's oddest trick was what he did during a game between the Knicks and the Boston Celtics. The Knicks would fall behind, then race back and almost tie the game. Then they would fall behind again.

What was coach Lapchick doing on the sidelines? He had taken off his jacket and was slowly ripping out the lining. He had the sleeves half torn off before he realized what he was doing.

How Soccer Began

The game we know as soccer is called football in most parts of the world. Whatever its name, it is among the oldest team sports known to man. About 2,500 years ago the Chinese had a game called *tsu chu,* which, loosely translated, means "kick a ball of leather with the foot." The game was often played for the emperor, and the players went after the ball—and each other—ferociously. The winners received handsome gifts, but the leader of the losing team was sometimes whipped.

The Romans played a game they called *harpastium.* The "ball" was the inflated bladder of an animal, which was kicked, pushed, carried, batted and punched toward some kind of a marker that served as a goal.

The Romans may have brought kicking games to England. But they don't appear again in history until centuries after the Romans had left the British Isles. In the 800s, some warlike Danish tribes raided the English stronghold of Kingston (some historians say it was really another stronghold called Chester). The British withstood the attacks of the Danes, and finally reinforcements arrived from London. In the battle that followed, the Danish leader was killed. According to the story, his head was cut off and the British soldiers kicked it all over the village. The victory was achieved on Shrove Tuesday (the day before the beginning of Lent), and the day became a kind of national holiday. Football was a special event on Shrove Tuesday (just as American football has become a special event on New Year's Day). Naturally, a human head was not used; a shoemaker made a ball out of leather. Whole villages played at once. There were few rules but a lot of kicking, punching and wrestling.

In parts of Scotland a different kind of football was played. It was called *melleys.* Teams of married women played teams of unmarried women. Almost always the married women won, beating up their unmarried rivals in the process.

British football became so popular that it interfered with the Anglo-Scottish War of 1297. The soldiers stationed in Lancaster had a football feud going with the Scottish troops. How could they play the game if the players were killing each other with arrows or lances? In 1365, King Edward III banned the game completely. But no one could enforce the law. When soldiers weren't fighting, they were playing football.

Except that "playing" was hardly the proper word. Anything short of murder was allowed, including punching faces, kicking ribs, butting into stomachs—it was all "legal."

Slowly but surely the violence decreased. Toward the end of the 1700s such schools as Rugby and Eton were playing against each other. There were almost no standard rules. Each school invented rules to suit itself.

In the 1800s several kinds of football developed from the wild early game. One came to be known as Association Football, or "soccer" for short. Another, first played at Rugby School, was called rugby football. It was from rugby football—in which a player could carry the ball with his hands—that the American and Canadian versions of the sport developed. But all of these games look back to the bad old days when English soldiers kicked around the head of a dead enemy.

A Little Too Late

In 1923, New York Yankee scouts Paul Krichell and Bob Connery heard about a strapping young fellow who was playing baseball for Columbia University. They went to Columbia to watch the player in action. What they saw made their eyes pop. The young man smashed the ball on the nose, and sent it out of the playing field, across the street and onto the steps of the library building.

"What did you say his name is?" Connery asked Krichell.

"Lou Gehrig," was the reply. "He's a first baseman."

"Let's grab him before someone else does," declared Krichell. That very day they got a promise from Gehrig that he would sign with the Yankees after school was finished.

The Yankees' regular first baseman was a slick fielder named Wally Pipp. Before coming to the Yankees, Pipp had played for Detroit. He still had many friends on the Detroit team. One day a Detroit official telephoned Pipp.

"Wally," said the official, "we've heard about a young prospect at Columbia University. His name is Lou Gehrig. Do us a favor and look him over. If he's as good as they say, try to persuade him to sign with the Tigers."

Pipp agreed, and he too went to Columbia to watch Gehrig. Sure enough, the young man was slugging the ball all over the field. After the game Pipp stopped Gehrig as he was leaving the diamond.

"You're pretty good," Pipp said admiringly. "Have you thought about playing professional baseball? I can arrange a tryout with the Detroit Tigers."

"Yes, I have thought about turning pro," smiled Gehrig. "I've promised to join the New York Yankees."

Pipp gulped. "Look, I was trying to do you a favor. Do you know who I am?"

"Of course," Gehrig replied. "You're Wally Pipp and you play for the Yankees."

"Okay," Pipp nodded. "Now do me a favor. Forget you ever saw me. And don't tell anybody about this meeting."

Gehrig did not tell anyone that story for many years. But he did join the Yankees. One day when Wally Pipp was sick, Gehrig took his place, and from that moment on became the Yankees' regular first baseman. Pipp never did get his job back.

Pipp said later, "If only I'd have talked to Gehrig a couple of days earlier, maybe I could have persuaded him to join the Tigers. And I might have stayed on at first base with the Yankees. I was just a little too late."

Hillcrest Country Club in California has long been a favorite of entertainers. One hot August day, comedians George Burns and Harpo Marx came to the club to play a round of golf. The thermometer registered over a hundred degrees, and the two decided to play without their shirts.

But then the course officials heard about the shirtless golfers and rushed out to find them.

"It's in the rules," said one member of the committee. "Shirts must be worn at all times."

"Why?" demanded Burns. "We can go to a public beach without them."

"Rules are rules," was the firm reply. "You can't play without a shirt."

The comedians put their shirts back on and started to play. The officials went back to the clubhouse. A few minutes later, someone came rushing in with the news, "Burns and Marx are playing without their pants!"

Again the committee raced out on the course. Sure enough, Burns and Marx had their shirts on, but they had removed their pants and were playing in their undershorts.

"Are you crazy?" yelled a member of the committee. "You can't play without pants!"

Harpo Marx reminded the committee of their rule book. "It says we can't play without shirts. But show me the rule that says we can't play without pants."

The officials were licked and they knew it. There and then a new rule was made: All male players could take off their shirts, but they had to wear pants at all times.

PLAYING by the RULES

Who's Minding the Fort?

When European explorers first came to Ontario, Canada, they found the Indians there playing a peculiar game called *baggataway*. It was played with a kind of ball, and a net made of strips of animal skin on a stick. Because the stick looked like a bishop's cross, the French explorers called the sport *lacrosse*.

In a way baggataway wasn't a game at all, but a way to prepare for future hand-to-hand combat. Teams sometimes consisted of all the young men of a tribe. Sometimes they even wore war paint. Goals were various kinds of markers, and could be any distance apart. Occasionally, the game was played on horseback. The referees were medicine men whose decisions were final.

Soldiers watching the Indians play thought the tribesmen were slightly crazy, because they suffered painful injuries and broken bones playing that violent game. But it turned out to be the soldiers who were foolish, because baggataway helped the Indians win an important battle.

In 1763, Chief Pontiac of the Ottawas schemed to capture Fort Michilimackinac (now called Fort Mackinac). But the French garrison was too strong. However, Pontiac knew that the French soldiers liked to watch the Indians play baggataway. He asked permission to play a game on a large open field near the fort, and invited the French soldiers to watch.

As the game got under way, the soldiers opened the gates so that they could see the Indians better. During the wild play, the ball was thrown near the gates of the fort and some of the Indians chased after it. That was the secret signal!

The older Indians were sitting at the edge of the field quietly watching the game. But they were concealing tomahawks under their blankets. The young Ottawa braves grabbed the weapons and stormed the fort.

Historians do not agree on the final outcome of that battle. Some versions state that the garrison was overwhelmed, beaten by an early sporting event. Others say the attack was beaten off. But no matter which ending is true, the fort soon fell into the hands of Chief Pontiac and the Ottawas. And two hundred years later, the game of the Ottawas is still played.

One day Bob Hope was playing golf with Sam Goldwyn, the movie producer. On one hole Goldwyn missed an easy two-foot putt. He became so angry that he threw his putter in disgust and walked away. When nobody was looking, Hope picked up the club and stuck it into his own golf bag.

On the next hole, Hope, who was a fine golfer, used the putter Goldwyn had thrown away, and sank a 20-footer.

"That's very good," Goldwyn said. "Let me see that putter for a minute."

Goldwyn examined the club, took a few practice swings with it and said, "I like this club very much. Will you sell it to me?"

"Sure," Hope agreed. "It'll cost you fifty dollars."

Years later Sam Goldwyn found out that he had paid $50 for a club he had just thrown away.

PITCHER'S NIGHTMARE

In baseball there is no clock. A pro basketball game lasts 48 minutes; hockey and football games last 60 minutes. But, as the old saying goes, in baseball the game (or the inning) isn't over until the final out. A game on May 21, 1952, between the Cincinnati Reds and the Brooklyn Dodgers proved the old saying true.

Third baseman Billy Cox was the first Brooklyn batter in the first inning. He grounded out. Now there were only two outs left. But then the fun began. Shortstop Pee Wee Reese drew a walk from pitcher Ewell Blackwell, and Duke Snider powered a homer over the right-field scoreboard. Then Jackie Robinson hit a double to left, Andy Pafko walked, and George "Shotgun" Shuba singled. Robinson scored. The Dodgers were ahead, 3–0, and there were still two men on. It wasn't a good way for the Reds to start a game, but there was still time to save the situation. They sent Blackwell to the showers and brought Bud Byerly in to pitch.

The Dodgers tried a double steal, but it didn't work. Pafko was put out at third base—the second out of the inning. The Reds relaxed a little—only one more out was needed.

The next batter, Gil Hodges, walked. Rube Walker singled, and Shuba scored the Dodgers' fourth run. Chris Van

Cuyk, the Dodger pitcher, singled, scoring Hodges. Billy Cox, up for the second time in the inning, singled, scoring Walker. Reese singled, scoring Van Cuyk. Now it was 7–0, and the Reds changed pitchers again. Herm Wehmeier replaced Byerly.

Wehmeier couldn't get anyone out either. Snider walked to load the bases and Wehmeier hit Robinson with a pitch, forcing in a run. Pafko singled, driving in two more. Frank Smith came in to relieve Wehmeier. It was 10–0.

Smith walked his first batter, George Shuba, loading the bases again. Then he walked Hodges, forcing in another run. Walker singled, scoring two more. Then Van Cuyk singled, driving in the 14th run of the inning. Smith was pitching as poorly as the three earlier Reds pitchers, but there was no sense bringing in another pitcher now. The Reds would just have to play the inning to the bitter end.

Billy Cox came to bat for the third time and was hit by a pitch to reload the bases. Reese walked, forcing in run number 15. Finally, Smith got the ball over the plate often enough to strike out Snider and end the slaughter.

As the Dodgers took the field, sportswriters had a chance to review the statistics. It was almost unbelievable. The half-inning had lasted one hour. Twenty-one batters had gotten ten hits and seven walks, and two batters had been hit by a pitched ball. Fifteen runs had scored and three men were left on base.

The following day the *New York Times* printed some of the records Brooklyn had broken in that half-inning:
- Most runs scored in one inning (15)
- Most runs scored in the first inning (15)
- Most runs scored with two out (12)
- Most batters to bat in one inning (21)
- Most batters to reach base safely in a row (19)

This last record may be the most amazing of all. Only the first batter and the last had not gotten on base safely. The 19 batters in between had all made it—even the man who was put out on the basepaths for the second out. The *Times* confessed it couldn't be sure that 19 batters in a row was a record. But if any major league team ever did better, no one remembers the occasion.

Try, Try Again

The tournament at Wimbledon, England, is perhaps the most important in tennis. A victory there is a tremendous achievement. Jaroslav Drobny found out how tough the competition is at this most famous of tennis events.

Drobny first came to Wimbledon in 1938 as a 16-year-old ball boy. It was his dream to take the championship back to his native Czechoslovakia some day. But then the Germans invaded Drobny's homeland, and soon World War II was under way. After the war, the Communists came to power in Czechoslovakia and Drobny became an exile. From then on he lived wherever he could, usually in Egypt or England. Year after year he kept entering the Wimbledon tournament. Sometimes he reached the semi-finals, sometimes the finals. But somehow he always lost the big match.

In 1953 Drobny was 31 years old. He faced Budge Patty in one round, in a match that is still remembered at Wimbledon.

Drobny beat his younger American opponent in the first set, 8–6. The second set was an exhausting battle, which Patty finally won, 18–16. He took the third set as well, 6–3. The old man seemed to be finished. But Patty was getting tired too. And Drobny managed to eke out the fourth set, 8–6, to tie the match.

It was getting dark by then, but the referee insisted that they keep playing. Drobny had to change his dark glasses to a pair with pink lenses; they were really his reading glasses. Patty changed his socks because his feet were raw and blistered.

They played on and on and on. With the score at deuce Drobny felt terrific pains in his legs. He did not think he would be able to continue, but then he saw Patty was also in agony with leg cramps. The old-timer found the will to continue, and finally came through, beating Patty in the final set, 12–10. The match had lasted five hours, and was one of the most grueling in the tournament's history.

But the championship still eluded Drobny. The Swedish star Kurt Nielsen beat him the next time Old Drob took the court, ending his chances for 1953.

But 1954 was another year, and this year Drobny got all the way to the finals. His opponent was young Ken Rosewall.

It was another tough match. Drobny repeatedly fell behind and then caught up. At one point in the first set Rosewall had him down by 11–10, and it was set point. But Old Drob pulled it out, and went on to win, 13–11. The Australian won the second set, 6–4. Back came Drobny to win the third set, 6–2.

The fourth set was almost more than Drobny could bear. He was nearly 33 years old and no longer had the stamina to hold off the young upcoming challengers. This could well be his last real opportunity to win at Wimbledon.

Again it was the see-saw struggle. But Drobny was a desperate man. It was now or never. He broke through Rosewall's service and went on to win the set and the match, 9–7.

At long, long last Old Drob had achieved his dream of winning at Wimbledon.

COLD CASH

In the early days of hockey, a great feud developed between the Renfrew Millionaires and the Ottawa club. One of the reasons for the feud was a remark by Fred "Cyclone" Taylor of the Millionaires. He declared that it would be easy to score a goal on goalie Percy LeSueur even if he skated backward. Ottawa fans didn't like that. During one game they threw rotten fruit at Cyclone.

The owner of the Millionaires, M. J. O'Brien, decided to give his team some incentive to beat Ottawa. He offered $100 to the team for every goal it scored in the game, to be divided up equally among the players. Furthermore, the player who scored the goal would receive an additional $50.

O'Brien must not have realized how eager his players would be for the extra money. The Millionaires pounded Ottawa goalie LeSueur throughout the game. The final score was 17—2, and owner O'Brien had to pay out $2,550.

And Cyclone Taylor got double satisfaction. He scored one of the goals *while skating backward,* making good his boast.

MISMATCH

Sometimes colleges schedule games that are complete mismatches. One team has absolutely no chance to win. But never was a score so lopsided as in the game between Georgia Tech and Cumberland on October 7, 1916.

Tech was coached by the great Johnny Heisman, for whom the Heisman Trophy is named. Cumberland, a tiny school, located at Lebanon, Tennessee, had a total enrollment of only 178 students. The Cumberland team agreed to play only because Tech promised the team a cash guarantee—money that would help support future football at the school. But within a few minutes, the Cumberland players regretted they had ever come.

The slaughter began almost immediately. After one quarter, Tech had scored nine touchdowns and led 63–0. At the end of the half the score was 126–0.

Georgia Tech scored whenever and however they pleased. Once Ev Strupper, who scored six touchdowns in the game, ran the ball up to the goal line, then stopped and put the ball down.

He wanted his teammate, Canty Alexander, to carry the ball over the goal and get credit for a score.

After scoring 126 points in the first half, Georgia Tech let up a little and scored only 96 in the second half. The final score was 222–0.

Total statistics were forgotten after a while, but some numbers were kept. For instance, Tech rushed for 538 yards on the ground and never attempted a forward pass. The team ran back punts 220 yards. And place-kicker George Preas kicked 18 points-after-touchdown in a row.

As for Cumberland, not only did it fail to score but it even failed to make a first down. Some accounts claim that its longest gain was a 4-yard *loss* from the line of scrimmage! Things were so bad that when Cumberland quarterback Ed Edwards fumbled the snap from center, none of the Cumberland players wanted to pick it up.

"Pick it up! Pick it up!" hollered Edwards.

Fullback Len McDonald took one look at the charging Tech linemen and yelled back, "Pick it up yourself! You dropped it!"

SPECIAL HANDLING

Who says football players are rough all the time?

In 1920, Montana played Washington State. Montana's quarterback, Harry Adams, had injured his ankle in a previous game but begged to be allowed to play. The coach agreed, but he made it clear that Adams was not to run with the ball.

During the game a Washington State punt sailed over Adams's head. Adams, playing safety, limped back to retrieve the punt. By the time he picked up the ball, two Washington ends were eyeball-to-eyeball with him.

"Don't hit him, he's hurt!" yelled one of the ends. Whereupon both players gently lifted Adams off the ground and carefully laid him down on his back.

ANGER

William "Brickyard" Kennedy was a good pitcher for Brooklyn before the turn of the century, but he had a terrible temper. On July 31, 1897, Brickyard and Brooklyn were locked in a tight game against the Giants. Kennedy was having his troubles with umpire Hank O'Day. Finally, O'Day called a close decision against Brickyard, and the hot-tempered pitcher was so enraged that he threw the ball at the umpire. The ball missed its target, but there were runners on base. O'Day called the ball in play, and one runner scored before the catcher could get the ball. Brooklyn lost the game, 2–1.

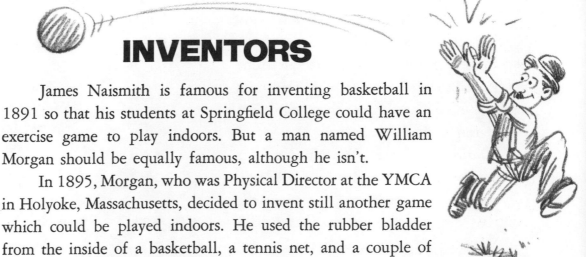

INVENTORS

James Naismith is famous for inventing basketball in 1891 so that his students at Springfield College could have an exercise game to play indoors. But a man named William Morgan should be equally famous, although he isn't.

In 1895, Morgan, who was Physical Director at the YMCA in Holyoke, Massachusetts, decided to invent still another game which could be played indoors. He used the rubber bladder from the inside of a basketball, a tennis net, and a couple of posts. Thus was born the game we now call volleyball!

"Cagers Defeat Foes 75–70"

Headlines like this appear in sports pages every day all winter. Readers soon recognize that a cager is a basketball player. Some readers may even understand that the word is used because "basketball team" is too long a term to fit in a headline. But very few have any idea *why* a basketball player is called a cager.

In the early days of basketball, teams used gymnasiums and meeting rooms that weren't designed for the game. Often there were pillars or posts set into the middle of the "court," and part of the game's strategy was built around the obstructions. But when the ball went out of bounds there was often a delay. The ball might roll down some steps and right out of the building. It might roll under rickety wooden bleachers. The players and spectators had to wait until someone retrieved the ball.

TEN MEN in a CAGE

According to one story, the first man to consider enclosing the court—so that the ball would always be in play—was Fred Padderatz of Trenton, New Jersey. Padderatz was a carpenter whose hobby was managing the Trenton basketball team. In order to speed up play, Padderatz built a chicken-wire cage eight feet high surrounding the court. Later, a few professional teams used a modified cage made of rope netting.

The cage did speed up play, but it had lots of disadvantages. It obstructed the view of the spectators. A more serious problem was the injuries the players got from banging into the chicken wire or netting—nasty scratches, bruises and burns. Before many years had passed, basketball gave up the enclosed court. But before it did, sportswriters had settled on a new, brief nickname for the game and its players. Cagers still play the cage game, although almost everyone has forgotten where the nickname came from.

Watch What You Sign

As usual, the world's greatest golfers entered the 1968 Masters Tournament at Augusta, Georgia. The line-up included Jack Nicklaus, Arnold Palmer, Gary Player, Tommy Aaron and a man from Argentina named Roberto de Vicenzo.

It was a tough tournament. At the end of the first round Billy Casper was in the lead with a score of 68. Two strokes behind were Tony Jacklin, Nicklaus, Aaron and de Vicenzo. But Casper couldn't hold the lead and soon dropped out of contention. At the end of the second round, Player and Don January were tied for the lead. De Vicenzo was three strokes behind. After the third round of 18 holes had been played, only three strokes separated eleven golfers. It was still anybody's tournament.

Roberto de Vicenzo began his drive toward the top with an eagle (2 under par) on the first hole of the last round. Then he birdied the next two holes, took an even par on each of the next four holes and got another birdie on the eighth hole.

One by one the competitors dropped behind, until, with two holes left to play, it was a toss-up between de Vicenzo and another golfer named Bob Goalby.

On the final hole, de Vicenzo seemed to have lost his magic. He took a bogey 5 (1 over par) when his putt failed to drop into the hole. But Goalby had bogeyed the previous hole. So, at the end of the match it appeared that Goalby and de Vicenzo were tied.

In golf, when two players are "paired," one player keeps score for the other. During the last round of the tournament, de Vicenzo had been paired with Tommy Aaron; de Vicenzo kept score for Aaron, and Aaron kept score for de Vicenzo.

Back on the seventeenth hole, de Vicenzo had scored a birdie, playing the hole in three strokes. But, for some unexplained reason, Aaron had written down 4. De Vicenzo was so happy with his tie that he did not add up the totals on his card. He signed it without looking.

The rules of golf are rigid. They say that once a competitor signs his card, no score may be changed. The officials saw that de Vicenzo's card showed his total for the last round was 66, not 65. They knew it was a wrong total, but there was nothing they could do because de Vicenzo had signed the card.

When de Vicenzo heard the news that he had lost the Masters with a single stroke of a pen, he slapped his forehead with his palm and muttered, "Stupid! Stupid!" Later, he told reporters, "I play golf all over the world for thirty years. Now all I think of is what a stupid I am to be so wrong in this wonderful tournament. I must be too old to win."

He never again came close in the Masters.

GOOD-BY, REF

The referee in hockey can throw a player out of a game. Once, however, a referee took himself out of a game instead.

In the early years of the century a Montreal team was playing Winnipeg in a Stanley Cup game. Referee J. A. Findlay imposed a penalty on a Montreal player. The Montreal players complained bitterly about the decision. After referee Findlay listened for a while, he announced that he had been "insulted." Findlay went home before anyone could stop him.

Some hockey officials jumped into a sleigh and went to Findlay's house. They coaxed and pleaded, and finally the referee agreed to return to the arena. By the time he got back, however, some of the Winnipeg players had already changed into street clothes and disappeared. The game was never completed.

AU REVOIR!

EXIT

Schaefer Steals the Show

He played for several major league teams, including the Cubs, Tigers, Senators and Indians, between 1901 and 1918. He could play the infield and the outfield, and once even tried his hand at pitching. His name was Germany Schaefer, and everybody, fans and players alike, thought he was just a little crazy.

Once when Germany was playing for the Senators, he was on first base. A teammate, Clyde Milan, was on third. The score was tied with two out in the ninth. Germany decided to try a double steal. He would go for second, and if the catcher threw the ball to second, Milan could score from third and win the game. Schaefer broke for second on the pitch, but the catcher held on to the ball. Germany slid in safely, but Milan had to hold his base.

To Germany, the double steal still seemed like a good idea. But where could he go now? Not to third, because Milan was already there. The logical answer was back to first. So on the next pitch he *stole first base.* The catcher was too surprised to make a throw, and Germany slid in safely. Now there was a lot of confusion. How could a player steal first base? And why would he want to, anyhow, since he was on second base when he started out?

There was no rule about stealing first from second. In fact, years earlier, a player named Harry Davis had done the same thing. But such silly running had to be stopped. Soon after Schaefer's theft, a new rule was passed that stated that if a player ran the bases backward, he was automatically out.

Earlier, when he was with the Tigers, Schaefer was called to pinch-hit one day. The Tigers were behind by a run, but had one runner on base. The crowd jeered when Germany came up —he wasn't famous as a consistent hitter. But he held up his hands for silence. Then he shouted, "Ladies and gentlemen, you see before you the world's greatest hitter. I shall now demonstrate."

And he promptly hit a home run! Instead of circling the bases normally, he raced to first and slid in. As he got up, he imitated the caller at a racetrack, shouting, "At the quarter, Schaefer is leading by a head." After sliding into second, he announced, "At the halfway point, it's Schaefer ahead by a length." When he slid into third he cried, "It's Germany Schaefer leading by a mile!"

When he touched home, he tipped his cap and shouted, "Ladies and gentlemen, that concludes my performance for today. I sincerely trust that you enjoyed it."

Determination

The pro scouts are fond of saying that most great stars show their athletic ability at an early age. Bobby Orr, for example, was an outstanding hockey prospect at the age of twelve. Mickey Lolich was pitching shutouts as a teen-ager in the Babe Ruth League. And there are many other examples. Yet sometimes a fumble-fingered youngster who moves as if he has two left feet turns out to be a superstar.

This is the story of one boy who couldn't seem to do anything right, at least in the beginning.

As a gawky teen-ager, the boy tried out for his freshman high school football team. Opposing players had a fine time running all over him. He tried out for the basketball team, and in three games failed to score a point. Baseball produced no better results. He was the first boy dropped from the squad.

Still determined, the boy came back out for basketball as a sophomore. But the team ran out of uniforms. Rather than get

one for him, the coach told him to forget about playing. The boy joined a team in a church league, but even facing other ordinary players, he couldn't get very far. His dribbling was poor, his passing was worse and his shots never went anywhere near the basket.

Still the boy was not discouraged. His father set up a hoop in the backyard, gave him a basketball and urged him to keep practicing.

His shooting did improve. Also, by the time he was a junior, he stood 6-foot-5. Noting the change, his high school coach made sure he found a uniform to fit the boy. The improvement continued, slowly, steadily. At graduation the young man was 6-foot-7 and good enough to receive several college scholarship offers. He chose Louisiana State University.

The LSU freshman coach found him eager to learn. The following summer, he took a job as counselor in a Wisconsin summer camp. There he met Ray Meyer, who had once coached the great George Mikan at DePaul. Meyer turned the young counselor into a fantastic shooter.

The rest of the story can be found in the NBA record book. The former clumsy oaf played eleven seasons with the St. Louis Hawks, and every sportswriter called him one of the greatest ever to play basketball at any time, in any league. By the time he retired, this superstar had scored a total of 20,880 points as a pro.

The player's name is Bob Pettit. He retired in 1965, but he is still in the record books with other all-time all-pro basketball players.

Beach Hockey

Years ago there was a hockey player in the NHL named Fern Gauthier. He played briefly for the New York Rangers and the Detroit Red Wings. Gauthier's problem was his shooting. It was so unreliable that someone wisecracked that Gauthier couldn't shoot the puck into the ocean.

Gauthier found out about the remark. He saw a chance to prove the joker wrong. The next time the Red Wings went to New York, he rounded up some photographers and they all took the subway to Coney Island.

As the photographers snapped away, Gauthier took a mighty swipe at the puck. He hit a glancing blow and it missed the water. He shot again, and the same thing happened.

Finally, Gauthier managed to smack the next three shots into the Atlantic Ocean.

Winning Villain

"Everyone loves a winner."

Most of the time this old saying is true. Knute Rockne was a colorful coach, and his Notre Dame team won a lot of games. The fans, the sportswriters and the players loved him dearly. Vince Lombardi was not so colorful, but his Green Bay Packers won a lot of games. The fans loved him, even if his players and many sportswriters were actually afraid of him.

But some coaches get their results from being hated. Gil Dobie was dour and drab. The fans, the sportswriters and nearly all his players hated him. But the records show that he was even more successful at winning games than Rockne and Lombardi.

Dobie became head coach at North Dakota Agricultural College in 1906. "Gloomy Gil," as he was later called by sportswriters, had an unbeatable team. Dobie's boys went through undefeated seasons in 1906 and 1907.

Then Dobie was hired by the University of Washington, where he earned his reputation as the most hated man in athletics. The first day of practice he barred everybody from the field. The mayor and the postmaster of Seattle wanted to get in, but Dobie wouldn't let them. A fistfight almost broke out.

Then he set about terrorizing the Washington players. "You are the dumbest, clumsiest excuses for football players I've ever seen," he snarled. One of the most popular students on campus was lineman Pete Tegtmier. Dobie growled at him, "You yellow-haired bum, you've got a yellow streak up your back as yellow as your dirty yellow hair!"

He never praised his players, even when they played their hearts out for him. During meetings with the team, none of the players were allowed to speak. He told quarterback Wee Coyle that he played like a man "devoid of brains." "I wouldn't even let you play," he said grimly, "if I didn't have so many cripples." Yet Coyle was one of the best football players in the Northwest.

No effort seemed to satisfy him. In 1915, Washington routed California, 72–0. Dobie didn't want his men to get too cocky—he ordered them to run 20 laps around the field.

Washington fans despised him. Spectators booed him openly and threw peanuts at him.

Dobie coached at Washington from 1908 through 1916, and in those years his teams *never lost a game!* Their overall record was 58 wins, no losses and 2 ties. Those nine undefeated seasons, added to the two at North Dakota Agricultural College, gave Dobie a total of *11 straight* undefeated seasons. It is unlikely that this record will ever be beaten. Later, at Cornell, he was undefeated for three more consecutive years, 1921–23.

But Dobie never mellowed and was never loved by very many of his players or fans. He proved that even a winner can be unloved if he is ill-tempered enough.

Don't Fall Down

According to hockey's early rules, a goalie was supposed to remain standing. The rule provided that if a goalie dropped down to the ice to block a shot, he was automatically fined two dollars. If he did it a second time in a game, he was fined three dollars and assessed a five-minute penalty. At that rate, modern goalies would be in the penalty box most of the time.

Short Stay

If there is a record for the shortest major league career by a pitcher, it surely belongs to a right-handed pitcher named Henry Heitman.

On July 27, 1918, Heitman started a game for the Brooklyn Dodgers. He faced the St. Louis Cardinals. The first four batters all hit safely. Heitman was sent to the showers. He promptly enlisted in the United States Navy and never played major league baseball again.

Marathon Match

Back in boxing's bare-knuckle days, there were comparatively few fans. It was considered a roughneck sport, fit only for rowdies. The first bout to attract widespread attention took place on April 17, 1860. It was an international match between Tom Sayers, the English champion, and John C. Heenan, the American titleholder.

At first glance it seemed to be no contest. Heenan was 25 years old, 6-foot-2 and 195 pounds. He was powerfully built and could drop an opponent with a single blow. Sayers was 34 years old and much smaller, weighing only 155 pounds. But he was quick and could punch. Sayers had defeated many rivals who were younger, stronger and heavier.

The fight was held in a meadow at Farnborough, near London. Among the fans were Prince Albert, husband of Queen Victoria, and William Makepeace Thackeray, the novelist. Also present were members of Parliament and many American sportsmen and newspaper reporters.

It was the prizes that made the match so important. The winner would receive $1,000 and a championship belt. The loser would get nothing. And there would be no question as to who was the winner, because the rules of boxing did not allow for a referee's decision.

A round was ended when a man was knocked down. The referee would then call out "Time!" The floored boxer was dragged to his corner and given first aid. At the end of 30 seconds the referee began to count. Both boxers had 8 seconds to come to a mark in the center of the ring (which is where the saying "Toe the mark" came from). If a man could not reach the mark he was declared the loser.

Even then there were some rules of fair play. A boxer was not permitted to butt, to gouge, or to hit below the belt. He could not hold and hit his opponent.

Sayers, the Englishman, drew first blood when he sent a sharp left to Heenan's nose. Heenan came back to score knockdowns in the second, third, fourth and fifth rounds. However, Sayers's lightning blows were getting through, and a few solid punches had closed Heenan's right eye.

Unfortunately, Sayers then ruptured a tendon in his right arm and soon it became useless as an effective weapon. So Heenan kept knocking Sayers down, and Sayers kept getting up. Soon both fighters were covered with each other's blood.

Sayers realized that the only way he could win was to close Heenan's other eye. But doing such damage with one arm seemed impossible even though Heenan was getting tired and couldn't go on much longer.

In the 37th round Heenan rushed out and seized Sayers in a headlock, then began to pound at his opponent's head and body. Sayers's supporters scrambled into the ring and rescued their man before he was killed. The referee had no alternative but to call the match a draw, even though everyone knew Heenan would have won sooner or later.

Both boxers were awarded belts and each was crowned champion of his country. But Sayers never fought again. Heenan fought only once more, and he lost to a fighter named Tom King.

SUDDEN SUB

One of the most popular baseball players of the 1880s was a catcher-outfielder named Michael Joseph "King" Kelly, who played for Cincinnati, Chicago, New York and Boston. Kelly was a good hitter and a great baserunner. When he tried to steal a base, his fans would shout, "Slide, Kelly, Slide!" This phrase was soon printed in the newspapers and made Kelly famous.

Kelly was also an alert ballplayer who was always looking for a way to get an advantage over the other team. One day, when he was sitting on the bench, an opposing batter hit a high foul ball that none of Kelly's teammates would be able to catch. Kelly leaped off the bench and went after the ball. At the same time he was shouting to the umpire, "Kelly now catching!"

Kelly caught the ball, but the umpire refused to allow the catch. "It's not against the rules," Kelly declared. "It says in the book that substitutions can be made at any time." The umpire still wouldn't call the batter out. But Kelly was right. That winter, a new rule was written into the book. Because of Kelly's alert play, the new rule said that a player could not enter the game while the ball was in play.

On Top of the World

His name was Alvin Anthony Kelly, and he was born in the Hell's Kitchen section of New York City in 1893. When he was orphaned at the age of 13, young Alvin went to sea. He claimed to have survived several ship sinkings, and that was supposedly how he got the name "Shipwreck" Kelly.

Some people said that the name "Shipwreck" came about in a different way. Kelly later became a boxer. He was knocked down so often, according to this story, that the fans began to sing out, "Sailor Kelly's shipwrecked again!"

Having failed as a fighter, Kelly got a job washing windows of tall office buildings. Later, he became a construction worker on skyscrapers. As Kelly leaped nimbly from one girder to another, he realized that he was not afraid of heights. He quit his job and went to Hollywood, where he obtained work as a stunt man.

One day in 1924, a Los Angeles theater owner hired Kelly to sit on a flagpole atop his theater. The owner thought such a stunt would be good publicity and attract crowds. He was right. People came from all over to see the man perched high up on a flagpole. And Shipwreck Kelly was off on a new career.

Soon flagpole-sitting became a fad. Shipwreck Kelly was the man who started it, and his picture began to appear often in the newspapers. He was collecting $100 a day for his "work."

Once up on the flagpole, Kelly could sit down on a kind of wooden disk with a cushion. He learned to take five-minute catnaps while sitting. He put his thumbs into holes in the pole so that if he began to waver, the sudden pain in his thumbs would jolt him awake. For standing he had a platform only eight inches square. There were ropes to keep him from stepping

off the platform, but nothing to keep him from toppling over. He could only inch around the platform in order to get comfortable.

Food and water and makeshift toilet facilities were hauled up by rope. Kelly had a blanket which he could hang up to afford him a little privacy.

By 1927 Shipwreck was nationally famous. But now there were so many flagpole-sitters that the police began to arrest them on charges of being a public nuisance. Kelly had his troubles, too. For one thing, many other men began to call themselves "Shipwreck Kelly." Kelly tried to stop them, but there were so many that he had to give up. Also, the police began to interfere. Once when he sat on a flagpole on top of a hotel, he drew such a huge crowd that he was slapped with a summons for blocking traffic. On another occasion he had to climb down because a policeman appeared with an axe and threatened to chop down the pole with Kelly still on top of it.

Wherever there was a pole, Kelly would climb it for a fee. He roosted on poles fastened to moving trains and trucks. He even tried a pole tied to an airplane—when the plane was in the air. Meanwhile, his agents sold pamphlets telling "the life story" of Shipwreck Kelly to astonished spectators.

By 1929 flagpole-sitting was something of a "new sport." That year Kelly sat on a pole over the old Madison Square Garden, and a reporter was hauled up by rope to interview him. Next came a job at a Baltimore amusement park. He stayed up for 23 days and finally came down to a roaring ovation.

Now others were joining the "fun." A 15-year-old boy named "Azie" Foreman went up a pole behind his house in

Baltimore and stayed there for ten days. Great crowds came to see the boy. When he finally climbed down, Azie was given a scroll by the Mayor of the city. While he was on the pole, Azie sang bits of a song called "The Flagpole Melody."

Soon Azie's record was broken by a younger boy named Jimmy Jones, also from Baltimore. Jimmy stayed aloft for twelve days, and practiced on the violin, too.

Next came young Billy Wentworth. Billy had the backing of his church. While he was up on the pole, the minister conducted preach-ins and hymn-sings.

Youngsters all over America, from the age of eight and up, were shinnying up flagpoles. Forgotten were the traditional games of summer, baseball and jump rope and hopscotch. It was crazy! Police were unable to do very much to stop the craze, but they did issue licenses to the youngsters who wanted to climb flagpoles. Then they went around checking on the ropes and rigging to determine if they were "safe."

Flagpole-sitting records do not mean very much. Even today some people spend weeks on top of poles to get into the record books. However, Shipwreck Kelly did establish a record of sorts. In 1930, he went up a pole and stayed there from June 21 to August 9, a total of 1,177 hours. He made a radio broadcast from the pole. And a pretty girl was hauled up to give him a haircut. The fee was $4.25, and he gave her a $5 bill. "Keep the change," he said loftily.

But as the 1930s arrived, flagpole-sitting began to die out. Some people, including Kelly, still went up from time to time, but nobody really cared.

On October 11, 1952, Shipwreck Kelly collapsed on the street and died of a heart attack. Under his arm was a scrapbook filled with faded clippings telling of his past glories. The police discovered that Shipwreck was on welfare and lived in a dingy furnished room. All his possessions were in a single duffel bag. Among them were his old ropes and pulleys, the unused tools of a forgotten and unemployed flagpole-sitter.

Boot the Ball

Bobby Jones was one of the greatest golfers ever, winning dozens of tournaments before he retired in 1930. One day in 1920, playing in the Southern Amateur Tournament at New Orleans, Jones found himself with an unexpected problem.

One of his drives landed inside an old shoe that lay on top of a workman's wheelbarrow. After deciding not to take a penalty for dropping the ball out of the shoe, he found a novel solution. *He played the shoe.*

The immortal Bobby walloped the shoe, which zoomed off the barrow. The ball flew out of the shoe and kept rolling, finally stopping only a few feet from the green. Jones chipped up to the green and holed out for a par.

GHOST TEAM

During a football season, newspapers and wire services depend on people calling in to tell them the scores of games played between small colleges. There is no other way they can get those results. They print the scores in the Sunday sports pages.

During the 1941 season, the *New York Times* received a call from a man who identified himself as Jerry Croyden. He said he was the publicity director for Plainfield Teachers College in New Jersey. Croyden said that undefeated Plainfield had just beaten Ingersoll, 13–0. It was their third straight win, their previous victims having been Winona (27–0) and Randolph Tech (35–0). Croyden also called in the score to a Philadelphia newspaper.

That was the beginning of a whole series of news stories. After Plainfield's fourth straight victory, Croyden began to send in stories about the team's players. The star halfback, John Chung, had scored 57 of the team's 98 points. Chung's accom-

plishments were written up in the *New York Post*. Next, Plainfield added two more victims, Chesterton and Scott. John Chung was running wild, averaging 9.3 yards per carry. Croyden said that Chung seemed to get his power from eating plates of rice between halves.

Suddenly Plainfield Teachers stopped playing football. Future games with Appalachian Tech and Harmony Teachers were canceled. Croyden explained that the team had disbanded, "due to flunkings in midterm examinations."

The November 17 issue of *Time* magazine had another reason why the games were called off. It was because they were never scheduled in the first place. In fact, there was no Plainfield Teachers College! There were no colleges called Ingersoll, or Harmony Teachers, or any of the schools Plainfield had supposedly beaten. The whole thing was a hoax.

Finally, Caswell Adams, a sportswriter on the *New York Herald Tribune,* discovered that Plainfield Teachers and its star halfback, John Chung, were invented by a stockbroker named Morris Newburger and a group of his friends at the Wall Street brokerage firm of Newburger, Loeb & Co. Newburger and his friends took turns playing the role of Jerry Croyden (there was no such person). They just wanted to have a little fun, so they had dreamed up a college, a winning football team, a few opponents and a great running back named John Chung.

Slow Finish

The final seconds of an auto race are always exciting. Speeding cars come flashing toward the finish line to take the checkered flag of victory, accelerators pressed to the floor. The noise, the blur of passing cars, and the cheers of the crowd all make the finish the most exciting moment of the race.

But that wasn't what happened to Dan Gurney in the first Daytona Continental, in 1962.

Gurney, driving a Lotus, had a comfortable lead over the second-place Ferrari. He was only a few seconds from crossing the finish line. Then suddenly, the Lotus slowed and stopped. Gurney's engine had gone dead.

Quickly, Gurney leaped out of his car and dashed over to the officials' stand. He consulted with them hurriedly, checking his time. Nodding, he ran back to his car, got in and tried to start the engine. It started briefly, roared, sputtered, then died again. But Gurney started the car again, and when the engine began to cough, he kept it in gear. The car inched forward.

Gurney's desperate strategy became apparent to the crowd. He was going to inch the car ahead by using the ignition starter!

Again and again Gurney turned the ignition on. Each time the Lotus lurched forward a little. The second-place Ferrari was streaking toward the finish at 180 miles an hour, Gurney was just going a foot or two at a time.

Dan Gurney just made it. He covered the final section of the race at approximately *one mile an hour,* crossing the finish only moments before the second-place Ferrari roared in going 180 times faster.

THE NOTHING PITCH

In 1941, Pittsburgh Pirates pitcher Truette "Rip" Sewell was deer hunting. A fellow hunter accidentally fired a shotgun in his direction and injured the big toe on Sewell's right foot. He recovered, but he had to change his pitching motion.

In the course of learning how to adapt his delivery, Sewell experimented with different grips and pitching speeds. One of his new pitches was a kind of "blooper." He gripped the seam of the ball with three fingers and lofted the ball toward the plate, giving it lots of backspin. Although the ball traveled slowly, it was spinning rapidly.

For a time Sewell did not throw the blooper in a regular game, but one day he did use it in an exhibition against Dick Wakefield of the Detroit Tigers. Sewell's delivery went up into the air about 15 feet, then dropped toward the plate. The ball looked as big as a grapefruit as it floated down toward the strike zone. Wakefield started to swing, held up, then finally swung and missed the ball completely.

Later, in the clubhouse, someone asked what kind of a pitch Sewell had thrown. Teammate Maurice Van Robays said, "That's an eephus ball."

"What's an eephus ball?" a reporter asked, puzzled.

"Eephus is nothing," Van Robays grinned. "And that's what that pitch is, nothing."

When Sewell decided to use the pitch in a real game, the umpires began to protest. They said it wasn't a normal pitch, and some of them said they would not call it a strike even if it came over the plate. Pittsburgh manager Frankie Frisch knew that the fans wanted to see the eephus ball, so he called on Bill Klem, the supervisor of all National League umpires. Klem watched Sewell throw the eephus and decided it was legal. He instructed all the umpires to allow Sewell to throw it.

Sewell won 21 games in 1942 and 21 again in 1943—with a little help from the eephus ball. Some of the better hitters could time their swing right and poke the ball into the outfield for a base hit. But most went crazy trying to judge the eephus pitch. By now Sewell was able to loft the pitch almost 25 feet into the air.

Then during the All-Star game of 1946, Ted Williams approached Sewell. "You wouldn't use that pitch in a game like this, would you, Rip?" he asked.

Sewell smiled. "I sure would, Ted. What's more, I'm going to throw it to you."

When Williams came to bat against Sewell in the eighth inning, the American League was leading by 8–0. The fans were bored. It hadn't been a very exciting game. Sewell went into his windup and threw the eephus ball. It floated to the plate looking as big as a basketball, so slow that it seemed even a grade-school kid could hit it. Williams swung and barely ticked the ball.

Again Sewell threw the eephus ball. Williams held his swing. It was outside. Then Sewell crossed Williams up by throwing a fastball right over the plate for strike two.

Once more Sewell wound up as if he were going to throw a fastball, but he threw the eephus pitch again. Williams was ready. He took a couple of steps forward, timed his swing, and smashed the ball high and far out of the park for a home run.

As Williams circled the bases, laughing, Sewell shouted, "You only hit it because I told you it was coming."

And perhaps that was so. Only a great hitter such as Ted Williams could really connect with Rip Sewell's pitch. According to Sewell, Williams was the only man ever to hit a home run off his famous eephus ball.

PHANTOM HOMER

Winning the Triple Crown is one of the great achievements in baseball. According to the record book, Joe "Ducky" Medwick won the honor in 1937. He led the league with a batting average of .374. He led the league in runs batted in, with 154. The only blemish on the record is that he was tied with Mel Ott of the New York Giants in home runs, with 31.

The strange thing is that Medwick actually hit 32 homers, but he got credit for only 31. On Sunday, June 6, Medwick's team, the St. Louis Cardinals, played a doubleheader in Philadelphia against the Phillies. A city curfew law stated that a ball game had to be finished by 6:30 P.M. If too few innings were played, the game would be postponed and played at a later date.

Early in the second game Medwick hit a home run. As curfew time neared, the Cardinals were leading. Phillies manager Jimmy Wilson knew what time it was. He also knew that if he stalled long enough, the umpires would be forced to call the game. Then maybe the Phillies could win when it was replayed.

When the Phillies came up, a batter walked out of the dugout swinging two bats, then tossed one away. He walked slowly toward the plate, stopped, and decided he had the wrong bat. Ever so slowly he ambled back to the bat rack and spent a couple of minutes selecting the "right" one. Then he walked slowly back to the plate. He brushed the dirt around with his feet and dug in.

The pitcher threw the ball. The batter stepped out and peered toward the third-base coach as if to get the sign. He nodded, wiped his hands on his pants, then dug in again.

Another pitch. Again the batter stepped out and looked for a sign. He reached down and picked up a handful of dirt, stared thoughtfully at the coach, and nodded.

Now the umpires took a hand in the proceedings. They knew what manager Wilson was up to and they warned him against delaying the game. Wilson began to argue.

The umpires called the game and walked off the field. Philadelphia had forfeited the contest to St. Louis.

In forfeited games, the victory counts in the standings of the clubs, but individual accomplishments do not. Officially no one comes to bat, no one gets a hit. So Medwick's home run was never entered in the record book.

The stalling tactics of Jimmy Wilson had cost Joe Medwick undisputed possession of baseball's coveted Triple Crown.

PEP TALK

Coaches use all kinds of psychology to lift the spirits of their players. Notre Dame football coach Knute Rockne once refused to sit with his team in the second half of a game. He sat in the stands, and the team was so fired up that it went out on the field and won.

One of the most unusual "pep talks" was delivered by coach Dana X. Bible during the Indiana-Nebraska football game of 1936.

Nebraska was losing, 9–0, at half time. Coach Bible looked scornfully around the dressing room and berated the players unmercifully.

"You don't have the desire to win!" he thundered. "You don't have the courage to fight back!" Then he said, "The first eleven players who go out that door will start the second half. The rest of you will sit on the bench."

Immediately, the fired-up team was on its feet trying to reach the door. But Bible got there first and barred the way.

"That's not good enough," he snarled. "You're not ready to play. You're not ready to win."

A slugging match followed. Teammates who really liked each other began to pummel at faces and heads, knocking each other down, then scrambling for the door. It became a free-for-all.

Finally eleven players did manage to squirm through. Bible put them on the field. And they beat Indiana, 14–9.

GIANT-KILLERS

Indiana has always been a basketball-crazy state. Hundreds of Hoosier teams play the game, in schools, church leagues and in the local Y's. Many of the teams come from small places, and some have overcome great odds to do well at the game. But perhaps no team ever overcame greater odds than the one from Wingate.

In November 1913, Wingate High decided to field a basketball team, and nobody thought much of that one way or another. Very few people in Indiana knew there was such a community as Wingate. It was hardly a dot on the map. If anyone asked where Wingate was, they were told it was near Crawfordsville, a town that was at least a little bigger.

What made Wingate's decision to play basketball so incredible was that the school had *only seven students,* all boys. All of them would be on the team. The new "team" had no coach and no home court. In order to practice, the boys had to use a tiny "crackerbox" gym at New Richmond, six miles away. They had to walk both ways.

From the very beginning, the Wingate boys stressed conditioning. They learned a few set plays and practiced them constantly. Then they put together a schedule of games. They were always the visiting team and had practically no rooters. Also, they had to get used to playing on courts that were far bigger than the one at New Richmond. All the odds were stacked against them.

TO THE PRACTICE COURT 6 MILES

But when they played, they won! They learned to play cautiously for fear of fouling out, and they paced themselves to keep from getting too tired. The seven players were rotated, so that the team always had at least one "fresh" player in the game.

The Wingate community was elated when the boys won the sectional championship. They could play in the state tournament if they chose to, but there were problems. They didn't have the money to travel to games elsewhere, and they couldn't offer a court of their own to play on. But the boys were determined to go all the way. They voted to compete in the state tournament. And they raised the money by themselves, asking their family, friends and neighbors for the precious dollars.

Many other teams had 15 or 20 players on their squads. Some people were saying that Wingate "had holes in their sneakers and bigger holes in their heads." But the seven boys of Wingate battled on, knocking other teams out of the tournament. And finally they beat South Bend for the state championship!

Was it just a fluke? Did they get lucky? No indeed! Because the following year those same boys, playing under the same conditions, came back to win the Indiana state championship again!

OPEN ODDITIES

In 1934 the U.S. Open golf tournament was held at Merion Course near Philadelphia. The eleventh hole, 370 yards long and par 4, was tricky. A creek cut across the fairway and then flowed alongside the green. In the fourth round of the tournament, Bobby Cruickshank, an excitable little Scotsman, was in contention for the lead. Then his drive on the eleventh hole landed in a divot.

He wanted to get over the creek, but he topped the ball. It was flying straight toward the water. Cruickshank was in agony. If the ball went into the creek, his chance to win the tournament would be over.

But the ball hit a rock in the creek and bounced up onto the green! Cruickshank was so happy that he threw his club into the air. A second later the club came crashing down on his head.

Cruickshank was not seriously injured and managed to par the eleventh hole. But he was shaken enough to lose his edge. He finished the tournament tied for third place.

Cruickshank's partner on that round was "Wiffy" Cox. On the very next hole, Wiffy got his share of bad luck. One of the spectators had taken off his coat and dropped it at the edge of the fairway. Cox got off a good drive, but the ball rolled right onto the coat. The spectator became flustered. He immediately snatched up his coat. Unfortunately, he also rolled the ball into the rough.

In 1950, during the same tournament at the same course, Lloyd Mangrum was in a tense playoff against Ben Hogan and George Fazio. On the sixteenth hole he was a single stroke behind Hogan, and his approach shot had landed about 18 feet from the cup.

As Mangrum walked up to the ball to play it, an insect landed on it. Mangrum watched the insect for a moment. Then he put down his putter to mark the ball's position. He picked up the ball, blew the insect away and put the ball down at the same spot. He holed out.

That move cost him any chance he might have had to overtake Hogan because he was penalized two strokes for lifting the ball while it was in play.

MAN AGAINST HORSE

Rodeo riders are a special breed of men. They are tough, hard-bitten cowboys who compete against the horses that are trying to kill them. Yet the men and the horses are not really enemies. The riders respect these animals, who go "sunfishing" high in the air and come down stiff-legged, because they cannot stand anyone up on their backs.

Pete Knight was probably the greatest saddle bronc rider of his day. He began to ride on bucking broncs when he was 15 years old, in 1919. His first ride in a small-time rodeo won him second money. Soon he was taking his turn in the big rodeo circuit. In 1924 he split first and second money at the big rodeo in Calgary. Sooner or later he got the best of every bronc on the circuit . . . all except one.

The horse's name was Midnight, and he was a 1,200-pound bundle of dynamite. Pete Knight tried to ride Midnight three times, but each time he couldn't stay on. His best effort was in 1932 at Cheyenne. Pete was aboard Midnight for seven seconds. But then the bronc let go with a shoulder whip that knocked his rider into the dust. Pete's friends tried to claim he stayed on for the full ten seconds, but the timer said no.

The great rivalry between man and horse ended in 1935. Midnight's legs began to go bad. Then in 1936 the great bucking bronco died. The rodeo riders who had never been able to stay up on the horse made sure Midnight was given a decent burial. They had a monument built to him in Plattsville, Colorado, and the poem on the monument expressed their respect and love for the ornery bronc.

> Underneath this sod lies a great bucking horse.
> There never lived a cowboy he couldn't toss.
> His name was Midnight, his coat black as coal.
> If there's a hoss heaven, please God, rest his soul.

Only a year later, Pete Knight also died. He was riding Duster, a particularly mean mount. The bucking bronc lost his footing and fell on his rider. Knight got to his feet. But then he collapsed and died before he reached the hospital. It was the end of one of the strangest sports rivalries.

Modern hockey players are supposed to be rugged men with great stamina. But hockey moves so fast that players spend only a couple of minutes at a time on the ice, then rest on the bench. Yet hockey was just as fast in the old days, and there was one player who *really* had stamina. During the 1922–23 season, Frankie Nighbor of Ottawa—nicknamed "The Pembroke Peach"—*played every minute of six consecutive games* at center. And he averaged a goal per game during his streak!

On December 7, 1967, John Ferguson of Montreal got into a fight with Gary Bergman of the Detroit Red Wings. Referee Art Skov imposed three minor penalties on Ferguson: for charging, high-sticking and slashing. Bergman was hit with two minor penalties for slashing and charging. Altogether, that one play accounted for five penalties.

UNDERHANDED VICTORY

For a long time most baseball players considered softball a sissy game. They insisted that it was much more difficult to hit a baseball than a softball. After all, a baseball is much smaller than a softball, and a baseball pitcher throws overhand, which means his pitches can be faster.

Then a few major leaguers met Eddie Feigner, softball's all-time greatest pitcher, and the big leaguers changed their mind about softball.

Feigner was so good that he didn't have to play with a full team behind him. He organized a "team" that he called *The King and His Court.* It consisted of four players: a catcher, a shortstop and a first baseman; they were the "court." Feigner, who did the pitching, was "the king." Feigner dreamed up all sorts of stunts. Sometimes he would move back near second base and pitch from there. Or he'd pitch blindfolded. He gained a great reputation as a showman, but few baseball players took him seriously.

Then on February 18, 1967, a softball game was played in Hollywood. One team consisted of major league baseball players. The other was composed of movie actors, including

James Garner, Don Adams and Steve Allen. The major leaguers did not know that Feigner had been slipped into the movie stars' line-up.

Feigner took the mound only when the Hollywood stars were in a bad spot. Then he strode to the rubber, and in succession struck out Willie Mays, Willie McCovey, Brooks Robinson, Roberto Clemente and Harmon Killebrew, five of baseball's greatest sluggers.

Feigner wasn't used to losing. When he faced the major leaguers his teams had won nearly 3,400 games against 300 defeats. Feigner himself had pitched 530 no-hitters, including 152 perfect games in which no opposing batter reached base safely.

Strangest of all, Feigner may have been the fastest pitcher ever. Bob Feller had been one of the fastest pitchers in major league history, and his fastball was once timed at just under 100 miles per hour. Feigner's fastball, pitched underhand, was timed at 104 miles per hour!

Georges the Carpenter

The hockey arena in the little town of Chicoutimi was filled with spectators. Fans had come from all over northern Quebec to see the exhibition game between the mighty Montreal Canadiens and their own local team.

The powerful Canadiens were very confident that this would be just a warm-up game. But when the action started, they began to think differently.

"Who's that fellow in the nets?" one Montreal player asked a fan.

"That's Georges," was the reply. "He is the local carpenter."

All night long the Canadiens fired shots on goal, but Georges the carpenter blocked the net. The Canadiens lost the game.

The Montreal coach lost no time signing the local carpenter who had helped defeat the great Montreal team. And that was how Georges Vezina came to hockey's major league. He played for 15 great years in Montreal. And when he died prematurely, the trophy awarded to the best goalie in the league was named in his honor.

Pennant Winner

Early in the 1911 baseball season, while the New York Giants were playing in St. Louis, a slender young man, dressed in his best suit, came to see manager John McGraw. His name was Charles V. Faust. He said that his middle initial stood for "Victory" and that a fortuneteller told him the Giants would win the pennant if Faust was on the team.

McGraw, like all old-time ballplayers, was superstitious. He handed Faust a glove and told him to go out on the mound and pitch a few balls to him. Faust, still in his suit, went into the weirdest windup anyone had ever seen. His arms went in circles, over his head, down across his body. His pitch had no speed at all.

McGraw called for a curve. He got a half-speed pitch that was as straight as a string. He called for a fastball, but got the same pitch. A change-up was no different. McGraw dropped his mitt and asked Faust to try his hand at batting.

By then some of the Giants were watching, and decided to have some fun with Faust. As Faust dug in at the plate, the batting-practice pitcher lobbed the ball right into the strike zone. Faust swung hard, and tapped an easy ground ball to the left side of the infield. The shortstop bobbled the ball on purpose, and while he was chasing it, Faust rounded first and headed for second.

As he slid into the bag, the second baseman purposely missed the throw. Faust got up and continued running. The third baseman also dropped the throw, and Faust dashed home, sliding in under the tag.

McGraw had a hunch that perhaps Faust might indeed be a kind of good-luck charm. He let the stranger travel with the team and gave him a uniform and spending money, but no contract. Faust didn't care. He warmed up every day, hoping that he would get into a game.

McGraw did let Faust play in two games after the pennant was won. He had to because the fans had heard about Faust and wanted to see the "good-luck charm" in action.

In one game Faust got the side out for an inning. Apparently the other team was trying hard *not* to score. And when Faust came to bat, there were already three outs, but he took his turn anyway. As before, his grounder was turned into a series of errors, and the young man went sliding into all the bases as the crowd cheered. He pitched in a second game and allowed a run.

But Faust was a good-luck charm. The Giants won the pennant in 1911, 1912 and 1913.

At the end of the 1913 season, Faust wasn't feeling well. He did not report to the Giants in 1914 because he was too sick. And in 1914 the "Miracle Boston Braves" unexpectedly won the National League pennant.

Faust never came back to the Giants. His illness was fatal, and he died the following year.

Oops!

The great Stan Mikita of the Chicago Black Hawks scored many goals in his career. But the first goal he ever scored in the National Hockey League was a freak. The puck never even touched his stick.

Teammate Bobby Hull came driving in on goal and took his shot from about 40 feet out. The puck hit Mikita's body and ricocheted past Ranger goalie Gump Worsley, right into the net.

MIRACLE DRIVE

Miracle Hills Golf Club in Omaha, Nebraska, is aptly named. On October 7, 1965, the record for the longest hole-in-one was established there.

Robert Mittera was the lucky player. At the age of 21 he was already a very good golfer, although he was not a big man at 5-foot-6 and 165 pounds. But he could drive nearly 250 yards on occasion.

The tenth hole at Miracle Hills was 444 yards long, with a drop-off at the 290-yard mark. A 50-mile-an-hour gust of wind sprang up as Mittera drove off the tee. The wind caught the ball and carried it over the drop-off. It rolled 154 yards more directly into the cup. A group of golfers playing ahead of Mittera saw the whole thing happen.

Cheers

On November 6, 1869, the first inter-collegiate football game was played. The contestants were Princeton and Rutgers. From that game came the basic idea of a cheering section.

Before the Princeton team journeyed to Rutgers, the players decided on some new strategy. During the game, they would let loose some blood-curdling yells that were intended to frighten the Rutgers players. They called this yell the Scarer.

Unfortunately, the strategy didn't work completely. The Rutgers players were taken aback by the yells, but the screaming also interfered with the Princeton team. It took too much breath and too much energy to keep yelling all the time. And everyone seemed distracted. Nobody knew when to yell and when to be quiet and play. Princeton lost that game, 6–4.

Still, the yelling seemed like a good idea, particularly if the players didn't have to do it. When Rutgers met Princeton again, some Princeton students got together and agreed to yell the Scarer so that the team could concentrate on playing football. It worked. Princeton won, 8–0. And since then college teams, as well as pro teams, have their own section of "cheerleaders."

On August 11, 1965, 12-year-old Karen Muir swam against 17-year-old Linda Ludgrove, who held the world's record in the backstroke. Karen, who was not yet a teen-ager, defeated the older girl *and* broke her world record, swimming the distance of 110 yards in 1 minute 8.7 seconds. Karen Muir became the youngest person to hold a world record in a major sports event.

SNEAKY SCORE

A player who runs back a kickoff or a punt for a touch-down usually needs more than a lucky break. He needs speed and quickness and the intelligence to follow his blockers and look for a hole in the defense.

But one time a fast halfback named Abner Haynes scored a touchdown on a punt just by using his head.

Haynes, who was playing for North Texas State College, dropped back to take a punt. But the kick was short, and the ball fell a few yards in front of him, took a high bounce, and rolled to a stop. Players from both teams gathered around the ball waiting for it to be whistled dead.

The referee started toward the group of players, but he had not yet blown his whistle. Casually, Haynes picked up the ball as if he were about to toss it to the referee. But instead he tucked it under his arm and went sprinting downfield. He was 20 yards away when the opposing team realized what he was doing. Haynes crossed the goal line untouched.

Naturally the other team protested, complaining that the ref was late blowing his whistle to end the play. But the referee declared that the play was perfectly legal, and the touchdown was allowed.

The Story of Slippery Rock

Many sports fans spend their lives rooting for teams that never play on television and that people in other parts of the country have never heard of. Only one small-college team is famous nationwide: Slippery Rock.

It all started in 1936. Every week the major news services picked the top ten college teams. But this season no one could decide which of the teams should be number one. Some thought it should be the University of Minnesota, others held out for the University of Pittsburgh. But one sportswriter thought the argument was foolish. To prove it, he wrote a story supporting Slippery Rock for number one. He wrote:

The Slippery Rock Rockets defeated West Virginia. West Virginia defeated Duquesne, 2–0. Duquesne beat Pitt, 7–0. Pitt defeated Notre Dame, 26–6. Notre Dame beat Minnesota, 6–0. Therefore, Slippery Rock has to be the number-one college team in the ratings.

The article was reprinted by newspapers all over the country, and got many laughs. Apparently readers enjoyed a story that poked fun at the big football schools and supported a small one. And they loved the name *Slippery Rock.* As a name for a typical small school it seemed almost too good to be true.

But there certainly was (and is) a college named Slippery Rock. It is a state college located in western Pennsylvania. According to legend, Slippery Rock got its name from a battle in 1779 between the Continental Army and the Seneca Indians.

The Senecas went on the warpath, raiding the towns and villages of the region. Then they attacked Fort Pitt (now Pittsburgh). The troops were hopelessly outnumbered and had to flee. During their flight they came to a creek that had many large flat, smooth rocks at its bottom.

The soldiers, wearing heavy boots, were able to keep their footing and managed to splash across the stream. The Indians, wearing smooth moccasins, slipped and fell on the rocks, enabling the soldiers to escape. Thus the spot was named Slippery Rock.

But today, Slippery Rock means small-college football. The team never has qualified for the top ten and probably never will. But its victories and defeats are important to its local fans. Forty years after that first Slippery Rock story sportscasters dutifully announce its scores. Once, during a game at the football-crazy University of Texas, the public address announcer gave other scores during the half-time break.

When he finished, someone in the crowd shouted, "What's the Slippery Rock score?" The cry was taken up at once. A hurried call was placed to Slippery Rock, and soon afterward came the news that the Rockets had won, which caused a mighty cheer.

In 1970, Texas announcer Wally Pryor gave the Slippery Rock score and suggested that the crowd might write to the small college and extend its congratulations over a winning season (Slippery Rock finished with a 6–3 record). Many people did write.

One letter, signed by 19 Texas students, read:

We, the students of Texas at Austin, wish to congratulate you and your team on a successful season. We keep in touch with your progress each year and are always pleased with your success. As far as we are concerned, we would rather see Slippery Rock in the Cotton Bowl than Notre Dame!

All by Himself

Ever hear of a one-man team? Pat McGee of St. Peter's High School in Fairmont, West Virginia, won a basketball game all by himself.

On March 16, 1937, the St. Peter's seniors played an intramural basketball game against the sophomores. With the score tied at 32–all, and four minutes and a few seconds left, all of Pat's teammates fouled out.

Standing alone, Pat McGee not only kept the sophomores from scoring but added three points to his team's total by sinking a basket from the floor and adding a foul shot. Final score: seniors 35, sophomores 32!

LUCKY DEFEAT

In 1942, Boston College was one of the most powerful football teams in America. With only one game left to play—against its archrival, Holy Cross—it was undefeated. Boston College had scored 249 points to the opposition's 19. If the Boston team defeated Holy Cross, it would go to the Sugar Bowl. Boston College alumni were so confident of victory that they were already talking of celebrating New Year's Eve in New Orleans, where the Sugar Bowl game would be played. And they had already scheduled a big party for the team at Boston's top night club.

But nobody had told Holy Cross about its rivals' plans. True, it had a mediocre 4–4–1 record, but anything can happen when rivals meet. Holy Cross had nothing to lose by taking chances, while Boston College had to be very careful.

For a while the game was close. Holy Cross scored first to take a 7–0 lead, but Boston College came right back with a touchdown. Although the point-after-touchdown failed, Boston trailed by only 7–6. That wasn't much of a lead against one of the top ten teams in the nation.

But Holy Cross kept up the pressure. By half time it led, 20–6. And in the second half, the game turned into a rout for Holy Cross. Boston College was humbled, 55–12.

It was the end of a dream. Some other team would go to the Sugar Bowl. The Boston College supporters canceled the party at the big night club, which was called the Cocoanut Grove. The players forgot about a night of celebration and went home instead.

That night a busboy at the Cocoanut Grove tried to replace a light bulb in one of the sockets. It was dark and he could not find the socket, so he lit a match. The match set fire to an artificial palm frond.

In moments the blaze was spreading —too fast to be stopped. The entire club turned into a raging inferno. About five hundred patrons were killed in that fire, and of the four hundred who managed to escape, many were badly burned. It was one of the worst fire disasters in American history.

The members of that Boston College team still talk about that date, November 28, 1942. Because they lost a football game to Holy Cross, they did not go to the Cocoanut Grove that night. A football defeat had saved their lives.

Spit It Out

In the early days of lacrosse, the ball was a great deal smaller than it is today (modern rules state that the ball must be about eight inches in circumference and weigh about five ounces). Early players learned to hide the ball in their mouths as they ran toward the goal. There was only one way to find out who had the ball, and that was to smack the opposing players across the body to make the ball pop out.

Good game~

Thanx, I enjoyed it.

On August 13, 1910, the Pittsburgh Pirates played the Brooklyn Dodgers. After nine innings the game was tied, but darkness stopped play. The nine-inning statistics showed that each team had scored 8 runs on 13 hits, and committed 2 errors. Both clubs had sent 38 men to the plate, both sets of fielders were credited with 27 put-outs and 12 assists. There were 5 strike-outs recorded against each team, and each side had given up 3 walks. It was the evenest game ever played.

Perfect Shot

His real name was Alvin C. Thomas, but he was known far and wide as "Titanic" Thompson. He was part gambler, part golfer—and all hustler.

When Titanic made a bet on a golf game, he always seemed to have a trick up his sleeve. Once he played against another gambler named Nick the Greek, who was also a very good golfer. Titanic was losing on the seventeenth hole, and so he made an offer to Nick the Greek which seemed too good to refuse.

"I'll bet you double or nothing, Nick," Titanic said. "I say I can hit eight silver dollars in a row with my pistol from a distance of twenty-five feet."

"You're on!" Nick replied, feeling certain that the trick was impossible.

But Titanic did it! He threw a silver dollar high in the air eight times, and hit each one with a shot from his pistol. Then he gave one of the coins to Nick as a souvenir.

Titanic's greatest "sucker bet" is still talked about to this day. He had lost some money in a dice game, and he bet the winner $2,500 that he could drive a golf ball 500 yards. Of course the offer was accepted.

It was a raw winter day. Titanic and his gambling friend drove to a golf course somewhere on New York's Long Island. On one hole there was a water hazard in the form of a lake. The lake had become frozen over.

Titanic teed up with the wind at his back and boomed a drive out onto the ice. The ball sailed, bounced, skidded, and rolled for what seemed like forever. It finally stopped almost *half a mile away!*

MOVIE FIGHT

Max Baer was a very popular boxer. He was handsome, full of fun, and a leading contender for the heavyweight championship. Movie producers thought it would be a fine idea to make a picture starring Baer. He was signed to play in a movie called *The Prizefighter and the Lady.*

In the movie, Baer was supposed to fight the real heavyweight champion, Primo Carnera. The champ was offered a good deal of money, and he agreed to act in the film with Baer. However, neither fighter wanted to "lose" the fight, even if it was only make-believe. The script was changed so that the fight would end in a draw.

The fighters put on a good show for the camera. After the picture was over, Baer called his manager, Ancil Hoffman. "I want you to get me a fight with that big guy," he said.

Hoffman shook his head. "You're not ready yet, Maxie. He's tough."

"I can beat him," Baer insisted.

"What makes you sure of that?" asked Hoffman.

"The way he moved in the movie," replied Baer. "I could have landed a couple of real haymakers, but I couldn't do that because it wasn't supposed to happen that way. Get me the fight, Ancil."

Reluctantly, Hoffman agreed. On June 4, 1934, the two boxers met with the heavyweight championship at stake. And for round after round, Baer kept knocking Carnera all over the ring. He floored the champ repeatedly. Finally Carnera had enough. He signaled to the referee that he wanted the fight stopped.

Ancil Hoffman was overjoyed. But he cautioned his new champ. "No more movie fights! We don't want someone else catching on to your tricks."

Losing to the Fans

There are many great traditional rivalries in college athletics. But perhaps the most famous is the football game between Army and Navy that takes place each year near the end of the season. Both service teams are always "up" for this game, and there have been numerous upsets. Yet, in two of the games it was the fans—not the players—who decided the outcome.

In 1946 Army had one of the finest teams in the history of college football. The backfield included a pair of legendary running backs, "Doc" Blanchard and Glenn Davis, known as "Mr. Inside and Mr. Outside." Going into the Navy game, the Cadets were undefeated. Navy, on the other hand, was ending a miserable season. After having beaten Villanova in the season's opener, Navy lost the next seven games in a row.

In the first half Davis and Blanchard each ran for a touchdown, and they scored a third time on a pass from Davis to Blanchard. The half ended with Army ahead, 21–6. Navy came charging out for the second half. It scored once in the third quarter and again early in the fourth quarter. But Navy missed the kick both times, so it trailed, 21–18.

Then near the end of the game Navy began shoving the tired, injured Army team back. It reached the Cadet 3-yard line with 90 seconds left to play.

The fans were so excited that they had come out of the stands and were massing along the sidelines. Some were actually standing on the playing area, but the ushers were unable to restrain them.

Two line smashes by Navy were stopped cold. Then a player came into the game with a play from the Navy coach, but he took too long explaining it and Navy was penalized five yards for delay of the game. So Navy had third down from their 8-yard line with time running out.

The play went toward the sidelines. Chased by an Army defender, the Navy ball-carrier disappeared into the crowd of spectators. Did he go out of bounds? If so, the clock would stop. Navy would have time for one more play. But nobody seemed to know if the play was out of bounds or not. The seconds kept ticking away, and the clock ran out before Navy could line up again. Army had won, 21–18. The Cadets—and the fans—beat a gallant Navy team.

Seventeen years later, in 1963, the fans would have another chance to help decide an Army-Navy game. This time Navy was favored, having lost only one game all season. Army had lost twice. Navy boasted a great quarterback named Roger Staubach, who had won the Heisman Trophy the year before as a junior.

But Army scored first. Sparked by their own fine quarterback, Carl "Rollie" Stichweh, the Cadets marched 59 yards, and Stichweh scored on a 10-yard run. Navy soon got its turn and at the half the game was tied at 7–all.

Early in the second half Navy scored and then stopped Army inside its own 10 with a fine goal-line stand. Early in the fourth quarter the Navy team scored a third touchdown to take a 21–7 lead.

There were ten minutes left to play. Little did Navy suspect that it would never get possession of the ball again.

Army took the kickoff and began to march steadily downfield. Finally quarterback Stichweh scored from the 1-yard line. Then he gambled on a 2-point conversion and made it. Navy's lead was cut to 21–15. A touchdown would tie the game and the extra point would win.

The Cadets tried an on-side kick. Once more Rollie Stichweh was the hero, recovering the ball to keep possession for Army. There were 6 minutes left on the clock.

Army kept shoving Navy backward as the clock ticked away. With a minute and a half left, Stichweh completed a pass to Navy's 7-yard line.

This time the fans stayed in their seats, but they were making a tremendous din. Three line plays put the ball on Navy's 2-yard line. It was fourth and goal.

Stichweh tried to bark out the signals, but his teammates could not hear him. Shaking his head, he looked helplessly at the officials. Then he held up his arms pleading with the crowd to be quiet. Nobody seemed to be paying him any attention. Before the ball was snapped, the gun went off. Navy had hung on, 21–15.

So, twice the fans made the big difference in an Army-Navy game. Would Navy have scored in the 1946 game if they had time to run off one more play? Would Army have scored in the 1963 game if they had time for one more play? Neither question will ever be answered. There is only one consolation for both teams: turnabout is fair play.

How far does a basketball player run during a game? Of course, the distance can vary greatly, but some years ago, Ben Peck, coach at Middlebury, Vermont, decided to find out. He put pedometers on the feet of his players.

The results: Overall, his team traveled a total of 24.01 miles, 11.97 in the first half and 12.04 in the second half. Forward Fred Lapham ran the farthest, 5.31 miles. The other forward, Tom Neidhart, covered 5.14 miles. Center Bob Adsit ran 4.25 miles. The guards averaged 2.66 miles each.

LONG GAME

It is always exciting to watch a perfect game in progress, whether the game is baseball or bowling. Barney Koralewski thought his attempt to bowl a perfect game would never end.

On March 22, 1934, Barney was entered in the Genesee Business House League in Buffalo, New York. As his friends and a number of spectators watched, Barney ran off eight strikes in a row. All other bowling lanes were deserted as everyone clustered around Barney. The tension was terrific.

Suddenly the lights went out!

People were lighting matches as they groped through the darkness. The owner of the bowling alley learned that all the wires were down because of an electrical storm. The lights would not go on again that night. The game would have to be continued the following week.

Bowling fans talked about Barney Koralewski's perfect game attempt all week. Would he tighten up? Would he be too nervous?

On March 29, Barney was back at the alley. Very calmly he threw four more strikes to complete his perfect game and win a gold medal from the American Bowling Congress. But it had taken him a week to bowl his perfect game.

WHO WON?

William Lawrence "Young" Stribling was a great boxer who earned the odd distinction of holding a world title for the shortest period of time.

In 1924, Stribling was 19 and was already a contender for the light heavyweight title. The champ was a tough fighter named Mike McTigue. A match was arranged between Stribling and McTigue.

The fight was held in Georgia, Stribling's home state. Naturally, the crowd rooted for their hometown boy. At the end of ten rugged rounds, referee Harry Ertle called the fight a draw. The crowd turned ugly. Realizing that he might be in danger, Ertle reversed himself and gave the decision to Stribling. Then, when he was safely on a train on his way out of Georgia, Ertle announced that *McTigue* had won the fight. Eventually, the bout went into the record books as "No Decision." But McTigue kept the title. Young Stribling held his championship only until the referee was out of danger.

The following year Stribling and McTigue tangled in a return match. Again they slugged it out ten rounds. And once more the bout ended in "No Decision." McTigue lost the championship that same year to another fighter. And Young Stribling never again won a world title.

Clothes Make the Player

Fashions in athletic clothing have changed in almost all sports. But in women's tennis the changes have been amazing.

In 1884, the first Ladies' Singles Championship was held at Worple Road, England. According to the records, the champion, Maud Watson, wore a very full skirt looped with drapery, which reached to her ankles. At least ten yards of cloth were used to make the complete dress. Its sleeves were long, and it was tight around the neck. No wonder Maud Watson couldn't cover much ground! No one argued that such a dress was good for tennis, but in those days women who allowed their ankles to be uncovered were considered very immodest.

In 1905 a special "tennis dress" made its appearance, but it wasn't much different from the one worn by Maud Watson. In 1909 both finalists wore full-length skirts, but the skirts were not so full and necklines were a little less confining. At least the players could move about and breathe a little more easily.

The first real break came about in 1914, when the French champion, Marguerite Broquedis, appeared on a court. She still wore an ankle-length skirt, but her blouse had short sleeves. She could swing her racket much more freely.

Then came 1919—and scandal! Another outstanding French champion, Suzanne Lenglen, wore a one-piece dress,

with a lower neckline and a skirt that reached only to her calf. The spectators were shocked. They said she looked "indecent." But Lenglen had no worries about tripping over her skirts. She won handily at Wimbledon, and soon other women began to dress in the same kind of outfit. Lenglen also wore colorful bandannas around her forehead and hair, a practice that would be controversial for 50 years.

In 1923 came another change. Helen Wills played tennis in a schoolgirl's uniform with a shorter skirt. She wore an "eye-shade" cap to shield her eyes from the sun.

Ten years later, in 1933, came another breakthrough. Helen Jacobs became the first world-class player to wear shorts on the court, and the excited buzzing could be heard throughout the stands. Oddly enough, men had been playing in shorts for years but nobody had thought anything of it. Gradually, the shorts became shorter. In the 1940s, "Gorgeous Gussie" Moran played with frilly lace sewn to her shorts. The shorts were covered by a nice topskirt, but Gussie became more famous for her costume than for her tennis.

Even then there was one more hurdle to get over in tennis clothing. Until the late 1960s major tournaments insisted that tennis clothes be white—only white. It was left to Billie Jean King, Rosemary Casals and other modern players to prove that pink or peach or beige outfits would not damage the game or the player.

Many fashions have a way of repeating. But no one can imagine that women will ever go back to copying the tennis dresses of the 1880s.

RACING THE RAIN

In 1950 the Brooklyn Dodgers were fighting for the National League pennant. Every game was important to them, and they couldn't afford to lose—not even to the weather.

One day the Dodgers were playing the Boston Braves in Boston. The Dodgers were ahead, but dark, threatening clouds were racing toward the park. The Braves were at bat in the bottom of the fifth inning. If the Dodgers could get three outs before the downpour, they would win. Otherwise the game would be called off and would have to be finished another day.

"Red" Barber, the Dodgers' great play-by-play radio announcer, was describing the action for Dodger fans back home. Sitting high in the Boston press box, he had a perfect view of

---

In 1906 a goalie named Fred Brophy of the Montreal Westmounts became the first one at his position to score a goal. He got possession of the puck near his own goal. While the opposing Quebec team stared, Brophy skated down the ice and shot the puck past goalie Paddy Moran. A couple of years later Brophy scored another goal!

the clouds. Soon he was announcing the game as if it were a race between the Dodger pitcher and the storm.

When the first Boston batter went out, Barber reported that the rain could be seen falling only twelve blocks away. It was moving quickly, but so was the Dodger pitcher. The downpour was only five blocks away when the second Boston batter went down. Now Boston's Sam Jethroe came to the plate, and Barber reported that the first drops of the rain were falling in left field.

Jethroe swung and hit a ground ball to shortstop Pee Wee Reese. According to Barber, the first drops were falling on the peak of Reese's cap as he scooped the ball up and gunned it over to first for the final out. Then both teams raced off the field just as the rain began to come down in buckets.

But the full five innings had been played. And the Dodgers won in what was probably the strangest dramatic moment Red Barber ever described.

In 1876 a pitcher named Joe Borden of Boston hurled the first no-hitter in the history of the National League. But Borden couldn't leave well enough alone. Soon after the game he changed his style of pitching and began to lose his stuff. Borden went steadily downhill, and by the end of the season he was no longer a pitcher—he was the club's groundkeeper.

Beating the Champ

A slim 16-year-old boy walked into the billiard parlor in Springfield, Massachusetts and looked around. There were very few people playing. One man in particular seemed to be just practicing, without much interest in what he was doing. The boy walked over to him.

"Want to play billiards?" he asked the man. "Want to play for money?"

The man nodded, amused.

"How about playing fifty points for ten dollars?" he continued.

The man agreed.

The boy won the right to shoot first. And then he ran off 50 straight points. The man never did get to shoot.

As the man paid the boy with a smile, he said, "You should become a professional billiards player. You're very good at it."

"Nope," said the boy. "Baseball is my game. I'm going to use this ten dollars for a bus ticket to Hartford. I'm going to get a tryout."

Years later, the two happened to bump into each other in New York City. The boy had grown to manhood, and he recognized his former billiards opponent.

"Hello," he greeted the older man. "I guess you don't remember me. We played billiards a long time ago in Springfield, Massachusetts. I beat you, 50–0."

"Oh, yes," the man smiled. "You said you wanted to become a baseball player. Say, I never did get your name."

"My name is Leo Durocher, and I did become a major league baseball player," the young man said with a grin. Durocher played for the world-champion St. Louis Cardinals in the 1930s and later managed for 25 years in the major leagues.

"Do you know who I am?" the older man asked.

"Sure," said Durocher. "I knew who you were when I challenged you."

The older man was Willie Hoppe, the world billiard champion, and probably the greatest who ever played the game. His loss to the brash 16-year-old ballplayer was one of the very few losses in his long career.

DREAM HOUSE

A golf game can really be the start of something big. In 1955, comedian Dick Shawn was playing at the Englewood (New Jersey) Country Club. One of his shots sliced off the course and bounced into a man's backyard. When Shawn went to see where his ball had landed, the owner of the house began to bawl him out.

But soon the shouting stopped, and the men began to talk on friendly terms. Shawn liked the house so well that he bought it for $50,000.

OUT OF BOUNDS

Little Star

Among the teams playing in the 1957 Little League World Series was one from Monterrey, Mexico. The star of that team was a youngster named Angel Macias. He was one of the most versatile young players ever seen. Angel could play all positions equally well. Not only was he the star pitcher, but he could pitch effectively both left-handed and right-handed. In one game he played first base and threw left-handed, then shifted to shortstop and threw right-handed.

Only his size was against him. Angel was small, much smaller than his teammates. But he was such a fine baseball player that his size was forgotten.

In the showdown game for the World Little League Championship, Angel pitched a *perfect game!* In six innings he struck out eleven batters. In Angel's hometown, church bells were rung. He was voted Mexico's outstanding athlete of the year in all sports, amateur or professional.

Being too old to continue in the Little League, Angel Macias joined the Colt League. He was equally successful there. In his years of Little League and Colt League pitching, Angel won 28 straight games. Every team in the major leagues waited impatiently for him to get taller. Finally the California Angels signed him to a contract.

But Angel never did grow enough. And his versatility counted for less. He was not quite good enough to make the major leagues at any position. The superstar of Little League ball turned out to be only a fair minor league outfielder.

Many pitchers have gone into the ninth inning working on a no-hitter, only to see it spoiled.

On April 7, 1918, Otis "Doc" Crandall of the Los Angeles Angels had a perfect game going against Salt Lake City. With two out in the ninth inning, not a man had reached base. Then Doc's brother, Karl Crandall, came to bat. He dumped a dinky base hit past the infield.

This is the only case on record where a pitcher's no-hitter was broken up by his own brother.

Where's the Ball?

Johnny Heisman, for whom the Heisman Trophy is named, was one of football's most inventive coaches. One of his oddest inventions was the old hidden-ball trick. One day in 1895, a player asked him if it was illegal to hide the ball during a play. He knew it wasn't against the rules, but how could it be done?

Two of Heisman's players at Auburn, Walt Shafer and "Tick" Tichenor, thought the ball could be hidden under a running back's jersey, and they helped devise a play. As the ball was snapped to Tichenor, the rest of the team would drop back and form a circle around him. Then Tichenor would slip the ball under his jersey, and he would drop to one knee. The team would run to the right and the defenders would follow them. Then Tichenor would get up and run the other way. Auburn tried the trick against Vanderbilt soon after and scored a touchdown with it.

Tighter uniforms and faster play have made the hidden-ball trick harder and harder to perform. The bizarre play is hardly ever used today.

A Matter of Life and Death

Stanislaus Cyganiewicz was an educated man. He was a lawyer, poet and musician, and he spoke eleven languages. He was also a professional wrestler, and in order to make his name easier to pronounce, he changed it to Zbysco.

For several years, Zbysko had a feud with another wrestler named Alex Aberg. Zbysko was from Poland, and Aberg was from Estonia. They had met twice in the ring, and both times had wrestled to a draw. During those matches the wrestlers had used a number of illegal holds, and as a result there was no love lost between them. To be truthful, they hated each other!

During World War I, the wrestlers agreed to another match, to be held in Petrograd, Russia. The spectators were to be mostly Russian soldiers, friends of Aberg. Aberg hated Zbysco so much that he began to spread rumors that his opponent was really a spy. Hadn't he graduated from the University of Vienna, which was in Austria, one of Russia's enemies? Was it normal for a man to speak so many languages? Why would he learn them all if he wasn't a spy? The Russian authorities believed Aberg. When Zbysco showed up he was arrested and thrown into prison.

On the day of the match Zbysco was taken into court. The judges gave him an incredible choice: If he won the match he would be given his purse and allowed to go free. If he lost, he would be executed as a spy. For Zbysco it was a terrible situation. Even if he did win, Aberg's friends might not let him get out of the ring and out of Russia.

The wrestlers tore into each other savagely. For 2 hours 43 minutes they strained against each other. Finally, Zbysco threw his opponent to the mat and pinned him.

110

As he stood in the ring and was handed the purse of gold coins, Zbysco could see the rage on the faces of the spectators. Calmly he reached into the pouch, took out the gold coins and threw them into the crowd.

Immediately, there was a mad scramble for the gold. Zbysco took advantage of the free-for-all to slip out of the arena and make his getaway.

Later, Zbysco went to America and became a nationally famous pro wrestler. When he had made enough money, he returned to his native land, bought a large piece of land and became a prosperous farmer.

EXIT

THE LONGEST RACE

In 1907, the automobile was new and auto racing was a new sport. Early races were held on hard sand beaches and between nearby cities on the dirt paths that passed for roads. But in that year a French newspaper, *Paris Matin,* sponsored an event that would be remembered long after the shorter contests were forgotten. It was to be a race from Peking, China, to Paris, France, a distance of almost nine thousand miles. The course led through Mongolia, across the Gobi Desert, into Siberia, over the Ural Mountains into Moscow, then down through Poland, Germany, Belgium and finally into France. Depots were erected along the route, stocked with extra tires, fuel and spare parts.

Five cars entered. The race began on June 10, 1907, and ended exactly two months later on August 10. The winning car was a four-cylinder Italia driven mostly by Prince Scipione Borghese of Italy. Two other cars arrived three weeks later.

The race was so successful that *Paris Matin* decided to sponsor another one, even longer. This time the starting point was New York City, and the finish line was in Paris. The cars were to head west, traveling almost around the world before reaching Paris. The American section of the race was organized by two American newspapers, the *New York Times* and the *Chicago Tribune.* According to the plans, cars would drive to California, take a boat to Alaska, drive north toward the Bering Strait, then take another boat to Russia.

112

On February 12, 1908, six cars moved to the starting line in Times Square, New York City.

One car was a German *Protos,* which had been built in 16 days by order of Kaiser Wilhelm, the German chief of state. It had six cylinders and a 40-horsepower engine, and could reach a speed of 70 miles per hour. It was easily the biggest car in the race.

Another car was an Italian *Brixia-Zust,* which had a 40-horsepower engine and could speed up to 60 miles per hour.

Then there were three French cars. One was a *De Dion-Bouton,* which had spiked tires for snow driving and a winch to pull itself out of snow or mud. The other French cars were a *Motobloc* and a *Sizaire-Naudin,* the smallest entry. Since it was so light, the designer thought it would not sink into the mud and snow as easily as the others.

The final entry was an American car, a *Thomas Flyer.* Because its body was aluminum, it was the second-lightest car in the race. But its four-cylinder, 60-horsepower engine was the most powerful.

It was cold and the sky was overcast when the race began. About 20 miles from the starting line the cars ran into a blizzard. They experienced all sorts of difficulties, going into ditches, snapping transmission chains, having radiators crack from the cold. There were some comical sidelights too. In one town the drivers of the Zust were fined three dollars for frightening a horse.

The first car to drop out was the French Sizaire-Naudin. While the car was still in New York State, a gear in the rear

SCREECH....

axle broke. There was no way to get a spare part to repair the damage.

All the car crews suffered incredible hardships. Once one of the Italian mechanics became so tired that he fell asleep while changing a tire. Food froze and was warmed by holding it over the steam of the radiator. When the cars got stuck in deep snow or mud they had to be hauled out by six or eight horses. It was not until February 26 that the lead car, the Flyer, reached Chicago. A day and a half later the Zust and the De Dion reached the Windy City. The Protos and Motobloc were far behind. In fact the Motobloc withdrew from the race at Cedar Rapids, Iowa, just two hundred miles beyond Chicago.

All the cars had narrow brushes with disaster. Crossing the Rockies, the Zust suddenly skidded to a stop. The road had been cut away by a landslide. A few feet more and the car would have plunged down a 150-foot cliff.

The Thomas Flyer reached San Francisco first and was shipped to Alaska. But the crew found it impossible to drive in the territory, for there were almost no roads to speak of. The car and crew returned to the United States. The race officials changed the route, leaving Alaska out and adding Japan instead. But the short scouting visit to Alaska cost the Americans their lead.

The Japanese section of the race was more difficult than expected. The road across Mount Fuji was so narrow that the cars could not steer around the hairpin turns; the crews had to get out and lift their cars around the bends. Bridges were so fragile that they almost collapsed under the weight of the cars.

From Japan the cars were shipped to Vladivostok, Russia. Oddly enough, at that point the owner of the De Dion decided to sell the car to a wealthy Chinese businessman. Now only three cars remained, the Thomas Flyer, Protos and Zust.

By now it was June. Spring rains had turned the Russian fields into mudholes. The American car overtook the Protos which was stuck in the mud. Sportingly, the Thomas Flyer crew pulled the German car free and continued on.

All the cars had broken down numerous times by then, but they forged onward, going through the wide Manchurian plains, across Siberia and the rest of Russia. The mechanics improvised beautifully when they could not find spare parts. Once the Zust crew made a new bearing from bullets melted over a small fire.

On July 26, the Protos drove into Paris and claimed victory, but the claim was denied. The Protos had been shipped across the Rockies by railroad instead of driving across, and it had not entered the Japanese section of the race at all. Officials said these omissions were worth 30 days of time. Thus, when the Thomas Flyer came in four days later, it was declared the winner by 26 days. It had traveled the distance in 166 days, or about five and a half months.

The Italian Zust had bad luck throughout the race. Once the Russians thought a crew member was a spy and detained the car. Another time the Zust frightened a horse, which then trampled a boy. That meant three days in prison. Between Berlin and Paris the car crashed into a ditch, and the crew was hospitalized.

Finally, on September 17, 1908, seven months and five days after the cars had left the starting line, the last car to finish the Great Race arrived in Paris.

RAINED OUT

Tennis grew up as a sport for rich and important people. It was played mostly at private clubs, and major tournaments were for amateurs only. If a player didn't have money, he or she had to struggle to find a good place to play and good competition to practice against.

So it was big news when the United States Lawn Tennis Association first admitted a poor black player from New York City to the National Championships at Forest Hills in 1950. Her name was Althea Gibson.

Althea was unknown. She had competed in Negro tournaments and National Indoor matches, but had never played in any of the really "important" tournaments. She was uncertain how well she would do against the nationally ranked players.

Althea won her first match, against Barbara Knapp of England, 6–2, 6–2. Then she had to play Louise Brough, a top player who had won three Wimbledon titles, the most important in tennis. The pressure was on. The tennis crowd would soon know how good young Althea Gibson was. When she came out on the court she could hear some of the fans shouting racial insults. She was nervous and played poorly. The first set went to Louise Brough, 6–1.

But Althea wasn't that bad. In the second set she settled down, winning 6–3. Suddenly spectators from other parts of the Forest Hills club arrived to see if Althea could accomplish a tremendous upset by winning the third set and the match.

Brough won the first three games of the set, but Althea fought back hard. She pulled into a tie, and then went ahead, 7–6. She was just one game away from victory.

Then, at the height of the drama, a summer storm broke. Lightning flashed and thunder rolled. Everybody ran for shelter as the rain softened the delicate grass courts on which the match was being played. The match was postponed, to be finished the following day.

That was the undoing of Althea Gibson. She had a whole day to think—the pressure she was under as the first black player at Forest Hills, the skill and experience of her opponent, the insults shouted by the fans.

Louise Brough came back the next day full of confidence. Playing a fine, steady game she tied the score, then forged ahead to win the match in three straight games.

Althea Gibson won the tournament at Forest Hills a few years later and she won at Wimbledon, too. But tennis fans still remember the day a thunderstorm robbed her of a great upset.

KING for a Day

Comedian Groucho Marx always loved to play golf. Unfortunately he wasn't very good at it. In his best days he never managed to break 90.

However, one day, while playing at the Brae Burn Country Club outside Boston, he got lucky. He took a mighty swipe at the ball and got a hole-in-one.

The next day, the *Boston Globe* reported Groucho's feat. The newspaper also printed three photographs side by side: on either side were Bobby Jones and Walter Hagen, the greatest golfers of the era. In the middle was Groucho. Under the pictures was the caption "Groucho Joins the Immortals."

When Groucho showed up at Brae Burn the next day, newspaper reporters followed him around from hole to hole. Ordinarily, Groucho could handle any situation, but for some reason he was nervous. When he came to the hole that he had made in one shot, Groucho blew up completely. He hacked and whacked and clubbed away, and he finally put the ball in the hole on his 22nd shot.

The next day the *Globe* again printed the pictures of Bobby Jones and Walter Hagen. But in the middle, the spot where Groucho's picture had been, there was a blank space. This time the caption read: "Groucho Leaves the Immortals."

What's in a Name?

One of the most famous of all poems is "Casey at the Bat," which was written by Ernest Thayer. It has been read by millions, and recited by dozens of actors. In the poem, Casey, a great slugger, comes to bat with his team behind in the ninth inning. There are two out and runners on base. Casey can win the game with a home run. But he strikes out.

A great deal is known about Casey's team from Mudville. The poem names and describes the four batters ahead of Casey —Cooney, Barrows, Flynn and Jimmy Blake.

The poet didn't pay much attention to the other team, however. The pitcher who faced down "the Mighty Casey" and struck him out is never even given a name.

GRUNT!

119

Time

How much action does a sports fan get for his money? A few years ago a man named W. Nicholas Kerbway decided to find out with the aid of a stopwatch.

First he timed the action in several Detroit Tigers baseball games. The stopwatch was set moving on each pitch, and then stopped when the catcher returned the ball to the pitcher. On a hit ball, the watch ran until the play was over.

In four Tigers games, the action took a total of 43 minutes 27 seconds, an average of less than 11 minutes per game.

Then Kerbway used the same stopwatch methods to measure the action time in football games. Kerbway found that there were 13 minutes 20 seconds of action in a pro game, 11 minutes 45 seconds in a college game, and 9 minutes 20 seconds in a high school game.

If Kerbway had continued his researches, he would have found higher figures for such sports as basketball, hockey and soccer where the ball (or puck) is in play for longer periods of time. And he would have found at least one sport with even less action time than high school football. In golf, the ball is in play for only a few seconds on each shot!

No Goalie Needed

When a team is losing in the final moments of a hockey game, it is quite common to see the goalie pulled out of the game and replaced by a third forward. Then six offensive men go storming down the ice trying to tie the score. Pulling the goalie sometimes works, but it often backfires, too. If the defending team can get a shot on the empty goal, it can just about end the game.

In 1950, Babe Pratt, a legendary player in his younger days, was coach of New Westminster in the old Pacific Coast Hockey League. One night New Westminster was losing to Vancouver, 6–2, with 14 minutes left to play. Pratt realized that his goalie wasn't helping the team, so he took him out of the game and replaced him with an offensive man.

The fans thought he was crazy, but Pratt felt he had nothing to lose. For most of the remaining minutes there was no goalie in the New Westminster net. Luckily, New Westminster was tremendously successful controlling the puck. In 14 minutes without a goalie, they allowed *no* goals and scored four themselves, to tie up the game, 6–6.

HELP!

Does friendship or baseball come first?

One day in a Southern League game a batter for Knoxville smashed a long, high fly to center field. Arnie Moser, the center fielder for Nashville, ran all the way to the scoreboard. The ball was over Moser's head, and he leaped for it but missed. The ball hit the scoreboard and came down. Moser hit the scoreboard but did not come down. His belt had caught on a wooden peg, and he was hanging helplessly on the wall, unable to chase the ball and get it back to the infield.

Moser's teammate left fielder Oris Hockett came racing over to back up the play.

"I'm stuck! Get me down!" yelled Moser.

Hockett looked up at his friend, looked for the ball, and looked at the runner rounding second base. He had to make a choice quickly.

"Get me down!" yelled Moser again.

"Wait a minute!" hollered Hockett. He picked up the ball and threw it back to the infield to keep the runner from scoring. Only then did he go back to the fence and help get Arnie Moser off the scoreboard peg.

TEAMWORK

What happens when a team doesn't like one of their own players? Pitcher Johnny "Phenomenal" Smith of Brooklyn found out that it doesn't pay to be too cocky.

Smith was a rookie, and he boasted all the time. On June 17, 1885, when Smith was pitching, his teammates decided to teach him a lesson. They committed 20 errors and Brooklyn lost, 18–5.

Phenomenal Smith was angry, but Brooklyn club president Charles Byrnes was even angrier. He threatened to fire every player on the team if they tried such a stunt again. The following day Brooklyn won. They committed no errors.

THE CURSE

Pete Muldoon was the coach of the Chicago Black Hawks in 1927, and the team did fairly well. But club owner Fred McLaughlin decided to get a new coach. Angered, Muldoon put his personal hex on the Black Hawks. He said the team would never win the Stanley Cup.

When 25 years passed and the Hawks had still never won the Cup, Muldoon's words were remembered. Perhaps he had really laid a curse on the team!

Never is a long time, however, and the Black Hawks did finally win the Stanley Cup and break "Muldoon's Curse" in 1962. But Muldoon had nothing to be ashamed of. It took Chicago exactly 35 years to break the jinx.

DOUBLE-TAKE

Gene Sarazen once took a tour to the Philippine Islands, where he had a match scheduled for the day after he got off the boat. But, when he checked into his hotel and examined his clothing, Sarazen found that his golf outfits were soiled and out of press. Sarazen prided himself on dressing in the height of style. He could not possibly go onto a golf course wearing dirty clothing. So he called for valet service, and a few minutes later, he heard a knock at his door. He opened it to find a beautiful young woman smiling at him.

"I need these clothes clean right away," Sarazen said, not sure she understood him. "Clean. You know what I mean?"

The woman smiled and nodded. He gave her the clothes. A short time later she was back with them. They were freshly washed and pressed. He gave her a large tip and she thanked him, still smiling.

The next morning, Sarazen was out practicing on Manila's beautiful Wack Wack Golf Course. A course official tapped him on the shoulder.

"Mr. Sarazen, I would like to introduce you to your opponent," he said. Sarazen looked. Behind the official stood the same woman he had given his clothes to!

It had been a mistake. She was a golfer who had just come to his room to meet him. When Sarazen mistook her for a valet service, she thought it would be funny if she washed his clothes and then played against him in a golf match.

She was a superb golfer. Sarazen just managed to beat her on the nine-hole course, 38–37. Her name was Dominga Capati, and she went on to become the Philippine women's champion five times.

Argument at Home Plate

In the year 1888, City College of New York played a baseball game against Manhattan College. The leading slugger of the CCNY team was a young man named Bernard Baruch. "Home Run Lefty" was his nickname—he could hit the ball a country mile.

Late in the game Baruch came to bat with the bases loaded, and he clouted a long fly over the center fielder's head. The runners scored, and Baruch raced around the bases trying to beat the throw. The pitcher was covering the plate, and it would be a close play. The pitcher got the throw, but Baruch slid in hard, knocking the ball from the pitcher's hand. Baruch had scored.

But there was a big argument between the teams. Manhattan players claimed Baruch was out. Soon the teams were fighting, and during the free-for-all someone hit Baruch over the head with a baseball bat. The blow was hard enough to damage his hearing permanently.

Bernard Baruch's ambition had been to go to the U.S. Military Academy after college. But his deafness made that impossible. Instead, he went into business and finance. In time Bernard Baruch became one of the richest men in the world and a trusted adviser to several presidents of the United States. West Point lost an officer, but America gained a great statesman, all because of an argument at home plate during a college baseball game.

LONG SHOT

During the Masters Tournament of 1935 Gene Sarazen belted one of the greatest golf shots ever seen.

Craig Wood, a magnificent golfer, started the last round of the Masters three strokes ahead. When he finished the round and went into the clubhouse at Augusta, Georgia, he was still three strokes up. Gene Sarazen was the only golfer with an outside chance to catch him.

Sarazen was about to play the fifteenth hole, one of the toughest at the Augusta National Course. It was a par-5 hole, with a 23-foot drop in elevation. Because a pond protected the green, the second shot was the most important. Even good golfers went into the water if they tried to get over the pond with a long drive on the second shot. The safest way to get a par was to drive off the tee, then pop the ball close to the pond.

After that, a chip shot would go onto the green. The golfer would putt twice and get his par.

But Sarazen knew he was losing, and could not afford to play it safe. He smashed a 300-yard drive straight down the fairway. Then, with a 4-wood, he swung to clear the pond.

The ball flew over the pond, bounced onto the green and kept rolling. The gallery crowd began to murmur, and then scream, as the ball kept rolling and rolling—right into the cup. Gene Sarazen had come across when the pressure was greatest. He had scored two on a par-5 hole—a *double eagle*.

After that, all he needed was a par on the last three holes to tie. He did it. And in the playoffs the next day he defeated Craig Wood to win the Masters Tournament.

ON THE ROAD

One of the hardest parts of being a professional athlete is the constant travel. No matter how carefully arrangements are made, they sometimes break down. Then the athletes must wait and wait and wait in planes, in airports, on buses, often without sleep and sometimes without food.

In 1955 the New York Knicks played a game in St. Louis against the St. Louis Hawks. Their next scheduled game was in Syracuse, New York. Their plane, an old twin-engined propeller model, was scheduled to carry them to Chicago for a connecting flight to Syracuse.

One of the players, Harry Gallatin, had parents who lived in St. Louis. They came to the airport to see him off, and they gave him a chocolate cake to take to his children in New York.

The weather was bad at Chicago. Planes were stacked up waiting to land. By the time the Knicks' plane touched down, after circling for two hours, the plane for Syracuse had departed. But the Knicks were told that another plane for Syracuse would be leaving in twenty minutes. So they stayed right in the airport close to the departure gate instead of hunting for a coffee shop.

But the plane did not take off in twenty minutes. Nor did it take off in an hour. By then it was snowing. Finally the Knicks got aboard. The plane was due to go to Syracuse all right, but first there would be stops at Cleveland, Buffalo and Rochester. Food would not be served until they took off from Buffalo.

The plane never stopped at Buffalo. The airport there was snowed in. Instead, it landed at Niagara Falls.

By then the Knicks were starving. They had not eaten lunch, and now there would be no dinner, either. The Niagara Falls airport had no real terminal then, just a few small offices and ticket counters. The players made a mad dash for the candy machines, but there wasn't much candy left in them. How could they hold out until Syracuse? And who knew when the plane would reach Syracuse anyway?

As the plane sat on the ground, the players suddenly remembered Harry Gallatin's chocolate cake. That was the only food on the plane.

"Hey, Gallatin," one player called out, "aren't you hungry?" Gallatin did not reply. The box of cake was under his seat, but it was meant for his children.

"Harry, we'll all die of hunger," another player yelled. Still Gallatin said nothing.

Finally a stewardess came to his seat holding a knife. "Your friends said you wanted to use this," she smiled sweetly.

Gallatin had a decision to make: his teammates or his children? Could he take away "grandma's cake" from them? He decided he had to do it. With a sigh, Harry Gallatin cut slices from the chocolate cake and passed them around.

It was late at night when the New York Knicks finally reached downtown Syracuse. The only place open was a small cafeteria, and all they had to serve was ham or bacon and eggs. But the players would have eaten the silverware by then.

Like a Duffer

Pro golfers are under great pressure in the big tournaments. One hook or slice, a misplaced divot that stops a rolling ball, or an unexpected cough or sneeze by a watching fan can mean the difference between winning or losing a match. The difference between first and second place can mean several thousand dollars.

One of the coolest of all pro golfers was Sammy Snead. He always seemed relaxed on the course, smiling at friends, chatting with fellow golfers. Even when he was losing, he enjoyed playing. But once, when he was a young man just

On May 30, 1922, the St. Louis Cardinals and the Chicago Cubs played a doubleheader. In the first game Max Flack played in the outfield for the Cubs and Cliff Heathcote was in the Cardinal outfield. Between games they were traded. And so in the second game, Heathcote played in the Cub outfield, and Flack caught fly balls for the Cardinals.

128

coming into his own, he blew sky-high.

In 1939, Snead entered the National Open, which was played at the Spring Mill course in Philadelphia. As the players teed off for the final round, three golfers were tied for first place: Denny Shute, Craig Wood and Sammy Snead. Shute and Wood played early, and they finished the course still tied with totals of 284.

Snead was still on the course, about to play the seventeenth hole, when he heard their scores. His total so far was 274. Even if he bogeyed one of the holes and took nine shots for the two of them, he would still finish with 283 and win the tournament.

The good news seemed to make Sammy nervous. One of his shots on the seventeenth hooked, and by the time he sank the putt he had taken five strokes for a bogey. But he could still win if he shot a par 4 on the last hole.

It was then that Sammy Snead came unglued. With the National Open title within his grasp, the ordinarily cool, happy-go-lucky young man became just another Sunday hacker. His drive went into the rough. His second shot landed in a trap 125 yards from the green. He blasted out of the trap and the ball rolled into a furrow. Knowing it was all over, Snead began to blast away. His fourth shot landed in another trap. His fifth shot went onto the green 25 feet from the cup. He tapped at the ball and it stopped rolling 8 feet from the hole. He hit the ball again and it rolled past the hole. Finally, on his eighth shot, the ball went in. But he had lost long before.

Thirty-five years later Sammy Snead was still a relaxed, cool golfer. But when one of his fans would compliment him on his coolness under pressure, he would grin and reply, "Let me tell you about the National Open back in 1939. . . ."

Much has been written about football's first intercollegiate game between Princeton and Rutgers. But very little has been said about the first intercollegiate baseball game.

It was played on July 1, 1859. Amherst defeated Williams. The final score was 66–32!

Photo Finish

The Florida Stock Car Championship race of January 16, 1952, was one of the most exciting auto races in history. No race of any kind ever had a more spectacular finish.

There were 34 drivers lined up, at the start of the race, ready to go 50 laps around the Opa Locka Speedway. The last two drivers were Alan "Rags" Carter, driving a Dodge, and Edwin "Banjo" Matthews, in a Ford.

The cars moved slowly around the track. Bob Verlin, the official starter, waved his yellow-and-green flag, and the 34 contestants began to zoom forward.

Rags and Banjo were experienced drivers. As the race progressed, they moved past the other cars until Banjo was in the lead, and Rags was coming on fast. With five laps to go, Rags was right behind Banjo, the bumper of his Dodge almost touching Banjo's Ford.

Rags realized that if he was to pass Banjo, he had to go around him on the outside, a dangerous move. The track was slippery there, and besides, driving on the outside meant he had to cover a greater distance. But there was no other way. Jamming his foot on the accelerator, Rags swung wide, coming perilously close to the crash wall.

As the fans came to their feet, roaring, the two drivers fought it out. They were almost exactly even as they moved into the final lap. Then Rags tried a very old racing trick. He had seen a slower car driving around the inside edge of the track. If he could force Banjo behind that car, Banjo would be blocked off.

Rags steered his Dodge slightly to the left toward the inside of the track, forcing Banjo to ease off in the same direction. Banjo tried to keep going straight ahead but it was no use. Rags kept nudging him to the inside. The two cars raced side by side, bumping up against each other. Banjo would have to "thread the needle" between Rags and the slower car. With a burst of speed he got through, still deadlocked with Rags as the cars turned into the home stretch.

Suddenly Rags's right rear wheel scraped and caught the crash wall. His Dodge went spinning into Banjo's Ford, which also began to spin, going across the track and onto the infield grass.

Rags was out of control, flipping into the air. Then his front wheels caught in the wall, ripping the whole front axle off the Dodge's frame. The car came down on its steel top, skidding ahead—across the finish line! Only the roll bars and the safety belt saved Rags's life.

Rags Carter had crossed the finish without a front axle or wheels. And he had come in while skidding on his car's roof, back end first!

Up, Up and Away

One of man's great ambitions has always been to fly. The early thinkers about flight were just dreamers. Later came the practical-minded inventors and scientists who made the first workable airplanes and later developed rockets for space travel. But in between the dreamers and the scientists came the sportsman fliers.

The brothers Jacques and Joseph Montgolfier were paper manufacturers in Annonay, France. They discovered that when a small balloon of paper and linen was filled with hot air, it would float up into the sky. They called the contraptions aerostatic machines, and soon they had sent one to an altitude of about six hundred feet. But when they reported their experiment, hardly anyone believed them.

So the brothers made a large balloon, measuring 105 feet in circumference. On June 5, 1783, they filled the bag with smoke, closed it, and let it go in front of a large audience. It floated for about ten minutes, then fell into a field. Terrified people who saw it land thought it was an evil spirit and they slashed it to pieces. But at least this time there were witnesses.

On September 19, 1783, the Montgolfier brothers sent up a balloon carrying a sheep, a duck and a rooster. All the creatures landed safely. And after that they sent people up for short rides. This began the gentle sport of ballooning—and marked man's first success in getting off the ground.

The Five-Base Hit

Strange things happen in professional baseball, but even stranger things can happen in amateur sandlot ball. Harry Hardner was involved in one of the most peculiar plays possible in baseball.

Hardner's Walnut Street team played on a field in Milwaukee that had no fences. No matter how far the ball was hit, it was in play until the pitcher had it back in his glove. In one game Hardner got a fat pitch and drove it far over the outfielder's head. Hardner raced around the bags happily.

Just as Hardner crossed the plate, a teammate who was coaching at first began shouting, "Run to first! Run to first!" The teammate and the opponent's first baseman noticed that Hardner had failed to touch first on his way around the bases.

Tired as he was, Hardner took off for first just as the ball came in from the outfield. He slid hard into the bag just as the throw arrived. The umpire called him safe.

Hardner was given credit for a single. But his teammates always called it a five-base hit.

LOST IN A FOG

Are umpires really necessary? Don't be too sure.

On June 28, 1941, the Boston Braves were scheduled to face the Brooklyn Dodgers. But a short time before game time, Casey Stengel, the manager of the Braves, received a telegram. He showed it to Leo Durocher, the manager of the Dodgers.

It was from the umpiring crew. All three umpires were fogbound on a boat and would not arrive in time for the game.

Durocher scratched his head. He never got along well with umpires anyway. "What are they doing on a boat?" he asked. "They're supposed to be here umpiring a game."

"Beats me," agreed Casey. "But we've got a crowd in the stands. We can't call the game."

"Got any ideas?" inquired Durocher.

Stengel suggested that they start the game without umpires. "One of my men, Johnny Cooney, can umpire behind the plate for balls and strikes," he said. "Is that O.K. with you?"

Durocher readily agreed. He picked one of his team, Freddy Fitzsimmons, to umpire on the bases.

With Johnny Cooney of Boston and Fred Fitzsimmons of Brooklyn doing the umpiring, the game got under way. The fans had learned of the telegram and the plight of the umpires. They enjoyed the situation thoroughly.

The first inning passed without incident. The Dodgers never questioned Cooney's calls behind the plate, and Fitzsimmons had little to do on the basepaths. Before the second inning began, umpires Pinelli, Barlick and Ballanfant trotted onto the field. The fans greeted them with much laughter and mock foghorn calls. Cooney and Fitzsimmons retired from their umpiring chores.

Later, Casey Stengel remarked, "We didn't miss 'em. For all I cared that boat could've been fogbound all day."

Curve

For a long time many baseball fans have insisted there is no such thing as a curve ball. They claim the curve is an optical illusion. But a pitcher named Fred Goldsmith proved that a ball does curve, and he performed his feat almost a hundred years ago.

At the Capitoline Grounds in Brooklyn, Goldsmith staked three poles into the ground in a straight line. Then he threw a pitch that passed to the right of the first pole, the left of the second pole, and back to the right of the third pole.

In the old days of hockey, the referee had to *place* the puck on the ice between the sticks for a face-off. By the end of a game his hands and knuckles were often black and blue from the swishing of hockey sticks. In 1914 all the referees breathed a sigh of relief. A new rule permitted them to drop the puck between the sticks of the face-off players.

One Last Victory

Every major league pitcher dreams of winning 300 ball games in his career. It is almost impossible to achieve such a feat. In the history of baseball only 13 pitchers have reached that mark.

One of baseball's all-time greatest pitchers was Robert Moses "Lefty" Grove. He had a blazing fastball, and many batters swore they couldn't even see his pitches, let alone hit them. He pitched in the majors for 17 years, and in 8 of those years he won 20 or more games. One year he won 31.

Lefty had his share of arm trouble. On one occasion his pitching arm suddenly went numb; there was almost no pulse in the arm. But, after a while, his "dead" arm suddenly came back to life.

By 1941 Lefty had achieved 293 victories. But now he was 41 years old. His fastball had lost its hop and he had to rely on curves and control. Lefty saw his goal of 300 within reach, and he pitched his heart out trying to reach that magic number. By July he had a record of 6 wins and 4 losses.

His next victory, number 300, seemed to elude him. He lost a couple of tough games. Bobo Newsom beat him in a squeaker, 2–0. The Chicago White Sox defeated Lefty by a score of 4–3 in ten innings. And his cause seemed hopeless when he faced Cleveland in his next start. The Indians pounded him for a run in the second inning and three more in the fourth.

But Lefty hung in there, and his teammates, the Boston Red Sox, kept pecking away. At last the mighty Jimmy Foxx smashed a triple to score two runs, and then a home run put the Red Sox far ahead. Boston won, 10–5. Grove had made it!

Afterward, in the dressing room, Lefty was jubilant. When asked how much longer he would keep pitching, the old southpaw declared, "I'm going to win another 300. They couldn't be any harder than the first 300."

However, that was Lefty's final great moment. He never won another game, and at the end of the season he retired.

Fish Story

One day in 1934, six men went trolling for tuna in the waters off Liverpool, Nova Scotia. Suddenly one of the fishermen felt a hard tug at his line, and then the rod was almost torn from his hand. The battle was on!

Ordinarily, a fish bites at the bait, and may be hooked by the mouth, or even may swallow the bait and hook. Then it is a matter of fighting the fish and nosing it to the boat. But this monster was foul-hooked, meaning that the hook had become accidentally embedded in its body. It is very difficult to bring in a fish broadside, and in the case of a large fish, it is all but impossible.

The six men took turns at the rod. They fought the fish all day, all night, into the next day, into the next night. It took *62 hours* before they were able to land that huge fish. It weighed 792 pounds!

Not Against the Rules

Two of the smartest football coaches of all time were Percy Haughton of Harvard and "Pop" Warner, who coached at Carlisle Institute and later at Stanford.

In 1908 Warner's team from Carlisle was scheduled to play Harvard. The week before the Harvard game, Warner had used a clever trick to help defeat a strong Syracuse team. Carlisle players had pads sewn to their pants and jerseys. The pads were the same size, shape and color as a football, making it very difficult to tell which player had the football and which one was only pretending. When Carlisle started to practice on Harvard's field the day before the game, Haughton saw the football-like pads.

"That's not fair," said Haughton mildly.

"It's not against the rules," laughed Warner. "I can put anything I like on my players' jerseys."

But Haughton had a few tricks up his sleeve. Just before kickoff time, Warner and Haughton met on the field to pick out the game football. Warner reached into the bag of balls Haughton had brought and pulled one out.

It was red! Haughton had dyed all the balls crimson, the color of Harvard's jerseys.

"It's not against the rules," Haughton smiled. "A football doesn't have to be *brown*, does it?"

Warner walked back to the sidelines muttering to himself. Harvard won the game, 17–0.

TOUGH MATCH

In 1948, when Richard "Pancho" Gonzales first won the U.S. Singles Championship in tennis, Charles Passarell was a boy of four. In June 1969, Gonzales and Passarell faced each other at Wimbledon, the most important tournament in the game. At the age of 25, Passarell was a rising tennis player. Gonzales was "over the hill" at 41. But age seemed to make no difference as the older man and the younger man played one of the most thrilling matches in tennis history.

It was late in the afternoon when they began to play. Passarell had the lead, but he couldn't seem to put over the final shot that would take the set. (The tie-breaker had not yet been invented, so players had to keep going until one of them went ahead by two games.) Eleven times he had the veteran at set point, but Gonzales wouldn't give up. Finally, youth won out. Passarell unloaded a shot that Gonzales couldn't return, and he won the set, 24–22. That tied the record for the longest set ever played at Wimbledon.

Gonzales wanted the match called because it was getting dark, but the referee insisted that they keep playing. The second set was easier for Passarell. He won it, 6–1. Now it really was too dark and play was halted. The two men had been on the court for 2 hours 20 minutes.

Nobody expected old Pancho to make much of a showing

the next day. That first long set had taken too much out of him. Passarell had to win only one set to win the match. Gonzales needed three sets in a row.

But now it was Gonzales taking the lead, Gonzales at set point, except that he couldn't get the winning shots. Seven times he was at set point before he finally won, 16–14.

On went Pancho into the fourth set, and he had the easier time of it. But he was playing it smart, conserving his energy. When he couldn't get to the ball easily, he didn't even try for it, letting it go by. He moved only when he had to. And he won, 6–3, to tie the match.

Passarell took the lead in the deciding set. He had Gonzales down, 5–4; then 6–5; but the aging tennis star kept fighting back. With the score deadlocked at 9–9, Passarell finally broke. He double-faulted, then hit a return over the baseline. Gonzales was ahead. Masterfully, he won the next point and the set and the match, 11–9.

It was the longest match ever at Wimbledon, taking five hours and twelve minutes. The match also broke the Wimbledon record for number of games with 112. Although no one counted, it was estimated that each man served more than 350 times in this one match and the ball crossed the net more than 2,500 times.

Between June 1949 and June 1951, New York Yankee southpaw Eddie Lopat defeated the Cleveland Indians eleven times in a row. When Lopat faced the Indians on June 4, 1951, one Cleveland fan decided to break the streak. As Lopat took the mound, the fan jumped out of the stands and dropped a black cat at the pitcher's feet. The jinx worked. Lopat was pounded for five runs in the first inning, and the Indians went on to win, 8–2.

Sudden Death

Mel Hill wasn't exactly one of hockey's superstars. He played first for the New York Rangers, but they thought he was too small, and they let him go. The Boston Bruins took a chance on Hill. He scored only ten goals his first season, but he made the team as a substitute.

As luck would have it, Boston met the Rangers in the 1939 Stanley Cup playoffs. It was a rugged seven-game series.

The first game went into overtime. The winning goal was pumped into the net by Mel Hill.

Two nights later, the Rangers and Bruins went into another overtime game. Eight minutes into the extra period, Boston got the winning goal. It was scored by Mel Hill.

The final game was the toughest of all. The teams were tired, and after two overtime periods the score was still deadlocked. In the third overtime period, after the Bruins and Rangers had been playing for 108 minutes, Boston got the winner. Mel Hill had scored again!

As a result of those three overtime goals in one playoff series, the former Ranger reject got a nickname that stuck for the rest of his life. He was called "Sudden Death" Hill.

ICING

Hockey is a fast game with a lot of body contact and shots on goal. At least that is how the game should be played. Nearly always, it is. But not on December 8, 1931, and January 3, 1932.

The Boston Bruins and New York Americans both were weak teams that season. Neither of them took part in the Stanley Cup playoffs. They played each other on the dates mentioned above in two of the dullest games in the history of hockey.

In the first game, the Americans slammed the puck away into the Boston zone every time it came near their goal. There was no rule against this kind of play, which was called "icing the puck." So the Bruins had to chase the puck into their own zone and come back up the ice with it. The Americans shot the puck away a total of 61 times.

The next time the two teams played against each other, the Bruins decided to turn the tables. Now they poked the puck into the Americans' zone, a total of 87 times. In both games the fans booed the teams all night.

Luckily, the foolishness was not repeated. Just to make sure, the league introduced a new rule against "icing" in 1937.

HUFFING and PUFFING

Athletes pay a lot of attention to their "wind"—the ability to run and run without getting out of breath. But one athlete, a baseball player named Bert Haas, once used his wind to stop a run from scoring.

Haas was playing third base for the Montreal Royals of the International League during a 1940 game. The Jersey City Giants had a runner at third when batter Woody Jensen tried to start a suicide squeeze play. Jensen dropped a beautiful bunt toward third. The ball rolled slowly along just inside the foul line.

The runner at third ran for home, and Jensen sprinted for first. Bert Haas realized that he wouldn't be able to throw out the runner at either base. So he got down on his knees and began to blow the ball toward the foul line. It kept rolling fair, so he blew again and again, harder and harder.

"Keep blowing!" screamed the Montreal infielders.

Finally, just before the ball reached third base, it rolled foul. The runner had to go back to third, the batter back to the plate.

Strangely, Jersey City did not protest. But Frank Shaughnessy, president of the International League, thought he should say something.

With a twinkle in his eye, Shaughnessy proclaimed a new rule: "After this, no player is permitted to blow a ball foul."

OUT
OF THE
WOODS

Many years ago, a young man named Joe Kirkwood ran away from home in Sydney, Australia, to punch cattle in the outback country. He got a job on a large ranch. The owner of the ranch was a golf fan, and had built a three-hole "course" for himself on his property. That was where Kirkwood learned to play the game.

At first, all he did was retrieve the balls hit out to the tees and run back with them. Then, he began to hit the balls back to the ranch owner; Kirkwood's shots were better than the ranch owner's. The young cowboy kept practicing, and finally the owner suggested he enter some tournaments. Kirkwood won quite a few. Soon he became a golf pro at a country club near Sydney. It was there that he perfected his assortment of trick shots.

Then Kirkwood came to America and did quite well. But he won a kind of immortality while playing in the Texas Open in 1924, at the Brackenridge Golf Club.

Going into the last round, Kirkwood was leading, but only by a couple of strokes. On one tee shot he misjudged slightly. The ball landed a few feet from a group of trees, not far from a bubbling creek. Kirkwood surveyed the situation thoughtfully. If he tossed another ball out away from the trees, he would be penalized, and he couldn't afford to lose a stroke. There was absolutely no way to hit the ball over the trees toward the green.

Finally, Kirkwood made up his mind. He selected a 3-iron and took his stance, *facing the creek.* Then he banged the ball. It shot across the creek, then began to hook in a long, curving arc. The ball kept curving around until it was going almost back the way it had come. It bounced, hit the green and rolled to a stop a few feet from the pin! Kirkwood went on to win the match.

Those who saw him make that shot swore they would erect a monument in memory of that magnificent trick shot. The money was collected, and later the monument was placed down at the exact spot where Joe Kirkwood had hooked a golf ball over a creek, around a grove of trees and onto the green.

On June 2, 1952, a player named Sammy White came to bat for the Boston Red Sox as a pinch-hitter. White took two quick strikes. Then he was called back to the bench and pinch-hitter Bill Henry went to bat in his place. Henry fouled off a pitch, took a ball, then struck out. But because White had two strikes on him before he sat down, the strike-out was technically charged against him. Thus Sammy White struck out while sitting on the bench!

DOUBLE DISASTER

Virginia College is a small junior college located in Lynchburg, Virginia. It has about one hundred students. Once it was part of a league and played a regular basketball schedule, but money was tight and the school had to drop out of the league. However, just to keep the students interested and active in athletics, Virginia scheduled two games with Beckley College.

Beckley is also a junior college, with an enrollment of about a thousand students. It plays basketball against regular four-year colleges in the West Virginia Intercollegiate Athletic Conference. Beckley's coach, Joe Cook, knew nothing about Virginia College when he agreed to two games during the 1975–76 season. He was surprised when Virginia's twelve-man squad showed up with a student coach. Right after the opening center jump, coach Cook knew that the game was a ghastly mistake.

Beckley scored so often that the team became bewildered. It wasn't even a good workout. Beckley won by the outlandish score of 132–43.

Cook tried to call off the second game, but the Virginia team insisted on playing. Maybe the players wanted to prove that they were not as bad as the terrible score suggested. Reluctantly, Cook agreed to play a rematch.

It too was a disaster. With about four or five minutes left to play, the Beckley manager said to coach Cook, "Look, we're leading by 130 points!"

As Cook said later, it isn't often that a coach has a chance to hear those words. The final score was 166–30. The Virginia College team went home determined to stick to studies—and maybe to an occasional pick-up game.

Marching Song

One of the most colorful club owners in all of sports was George Preston Marshall, owner of the Washington Redskins football team from the 1930s to 1963. He entertained the Washington fans in many different ways. One of his pet projects was the Redskin Marching Band. A special song was written for them, called "Hail to the Redskins." The music was composed by a society bandleader named Barnee Breeskin. The words were written by Corinne Marshall, the owner's wife.

Then the Marshalls were divorced. Corinne Marshall kept the rights to the song, and years afterward they passed to a man named Ted Webb.

Many years later, the National Football League expanded to Dallas. As it happened, Ted Webb, the owner of the marching song, worked for millionaire Clint Murchison, who wanted to own the Dallas team. But Murchison needed the approval of the rest of the club owners, and George Preston Marshall refused.

Then Marshall learned that Murchison owned the rights to his beloved Redskin marching song. Murchison could *forbid* the Redskins to sing their own theme song.

No one knows for sure why George Preston Marshall changed his mind and voted for Murchison's ownership of the new team in Dallas. But as part of the deal he got back the rights to "Hail to the Redskins."

RAH!
RAH!

Lifting the Cup

A hockey fan is happiest when his team is winning the Stanley Cup. But when his team is losing in the playoffs, a fan may do some peculiar things.

During the 1962 playoffs, a rabid Montreal Canadiens rooter named Ken Kilander traveled to Chicago to see a play-off game between the Chicago Black Hawks and the Canadiens. By the third period Montreal was far behind and Kilander had had enough. Frustrated, he wandered into the lobby of the arena. There, in a glass case, was the Stanley Cup itself, which the Black Hawks had won the previous year.

Kilander pried open the case and lifted out the Cup. That alone was a great accomplishment, because it weighed about 150 pounds. He was staggering out of the arena when two ushers grabbed him. The police were called and Kilander found himself facing a judge.

"Your honor, I just couldn't stand it," Kilander explained. "I root for the Canadiens. That cup rightfully belongs in Montreal. Everyone knows they're the best team."

"The Cup belongs to the team that wins it," replied the judge.

The Black Hawks' management were understanding. They refused to press charges, and Kilander was released.

When the playoffs were over, the Stanley Cup moved halfway to Montreal, spending the year in Toronto's Maple Leaf Gardens. At least it was back in Canada, but chances are that Ken Kilander fretted until it returned all the way to Montreal.

LOVE finds a way

This is the cast of characters in the story: Lyle Bennett, a sophomore at Brigham Young University who worked in the college athletic office; Mary Shurtz, Lyle Bennett's girlfriend and a freshman at BYU; and Steve Siegel, whose hobby was hang-gliding.

Bennett was an inventive young man and wanted to propose to Mary in a novel way. He knew that Mary would be at the Brigham Young–Utah football game one Saturday in 1975, so he chose that day to ask her to marry him. The BYU cheering section used flashcards that formed huge designs and figures when viewed from across the field. Lyle Bennett had arranged with the organizers of the cheering section to have a special card trick done. During the half-time show the cards suddenly spelled out a message for only one person in the crowd: "Mary Shurtz, Will you marry me? Love, Lyle."

Meanwhile, Steve Siegel had a trick of his own in mind. He climbed up "Y" Mountain, near the Brigham Young stadium. During half time he strapped himself into his hang-gliding rig, took a running start down the mountain and soon was flying. He soared over the stadium, glided around for a while, then made a perfect landing on the field as the crowd cheered.

Lyle Bennett thought it was a fine glide. But he was unhappy he didn't know of Siegel's plans earlier. "If I had known he was going to do this," Bennett said later, "I'd have had him bring the ring."

Even without the ring, Mary Shurtz agreed to Bennett's flashcard proposal, and they were engaged to be married.

ABOUT THE AUTHOR
AND ILLUSTRATOR

HOWARD LISS has written more than a dozen sports books for young readers, including books of strange but true stories about baseball, basketball and hockey. He has also written Broadway musicals, comic strips and books for adults. He lives and works in New York City.

JOE MATHIEU is a busy illustrator of books for children. Among his popular titles are *Big Joe's Trailer Truck* and *Grover and the Everything in the Whole Wide World Museum.* He also does illustrations for magazines and has designed tee shirts and bed-sheets. Mr. Mathieu and his family live in Putnam, Connecticut.